The AWESOME Untold Story

Gary Alan Rothhaar

Copyright © 2023, 2024 Gary Alan Rothhaar.

All rights reserved. No part of this book may be reproduced, stored, or transmitted by any means—whether auditory, graphic, mechanical, or electronic—without written permission of both publisher and author, except in the case of brief excerpts used in critical articles and reviews. Unauthorized reproduction of any part of this work is illegal and is punishable by law.

Library of Congress Control Number: 2023911574

ISBN: 979-8-89031-940-1 (sc)
ISBN: 979-8-89031-941-8 (hc)
ISBN: 979-8-89031-942-5 (e)

Because of the dynamic nature of the Internet, any web addresses or links contained in this book may have changed since publication and may no longer be valid. The views expressed in this work are solely those of the author and do not necessarily reflect the views of the publisher, and the publisher hereby disclaims any responsibility for them.

One Galleria Blvd., Suite 1900, Metairie, LA 70001
(504) 702-6708

Contents

Book of Revelation: A Brief Overview 1
DANIEL Chapter 9 The 70th week of Daniel 9
~ Part One ~
First 3 ½ Years of Seven Year Tribulation 13
Rev. Ch. 1 John commissioned to write to 7 churches 15
Rev. Ch. 2 Letters to Churches 19
Rev. Ch. 3 Letters to the Churches 23
Rev. Ch. 4 John's Vision of Heaven 27
Rev. Ch. 5 The Book with 7 Seals 31
Rev. Ch. 6 Six of Seven Seals opened 35
Rev. Ch. 7 The 144,000 SEALED 41
Rev. Ch. 10 The Edible Book 45
Rev. Ch. 11 The TWO WITNESSES 47
MATTHEW Chapter 24
The Mt. Olivet Discourse 55
Rev. Ch. 12 THE WOMAN (Israel) 61
Rev. Ch. 13A Antichrist (beast) Revealed 65
Rev. Ch. 13 B The False Prophet 71
Rev. Ch. 14 A The "Wave" Offering 77
Rev. Ch. 14 B The Harvest of the Earth is Ripe 81
Rev. Ch. 19A The Marriage Supper of the Lamb 87
~Part Two~
Second 3 ½ Years of Seven Year Tribulation
   THE WRATH OF GOD 93
Rev. Ch. 8 Seventh Seal Opened 95
Rev. Ch. 9 Demons from Bottomless Pit, and Euphrates
   River 99
Rev. Ch. 15 Prelude to Seven Bowls Judgment 103
Rev. Ch. 16 Seven Bowls Judgment 105

Rev. Ch. 17 A Mystery Babylon..111
Rev. Ch. 17 B Mystery Babylon Continued 115
Rev. Ch. 18 The Fall of Babylon..119
Rev. Ch. 19 B Battle of Armageddon 121
Rev. Ch. 20 A Satan Arrested and Imprisoned 1000 years.. 125
Rev. Ch. 20 B Jesus Separates the Sheep from the Goats 129
Rev. Ch. 20 C What is the purpose of the 1000 year millennium?... 133
Rev. Ch. 20 D Satan Released a for Short Time 137
Rev. Ch. 20E The Great White Throne Judgment......... 141
Rev. Ch. 21 The New Heaven, New Earth, and New Jerusalem 145
Rev. Ch. 22 The River and Tree of Life 151

DEDICATION

I dedicate this publication to my Lord and Savior Jesus Christ for He is the one who forgave my sins, saved my soul, indwelled me with the Holy Spirit, revealed His word to me, and inspired the writing of this book. I would also like to thank my faithful friends and family members for their valuable support and advice during the writing of this book.

Gary Alan Rothhaar

PREFACE

While studying this presentation of Revelation, please have your Bible at hand so that you can read each verse and be familiar with its content before reading the related comments.

Gary admits that he doesn't have all the answers, and does not expect all readers to agree with everything written in this book. He only asks that readers complete the book, and keep an open mind to all of the biblical concepts that are presented. This book contains more than 500 biblical references to verify its scriptural accuracy.

AWESOME UNTOLD STORY
Teacher Friendly Version

Included in this ***Teacher Friendly Version*** of the Awesome Untold Story of the Revelation of Jesus Christ is a seven year period of time when a series of terrible events will occur worldwide. The purpose of the seven years of tribulation is to awaken the Jewish people as to whom their true Messiah is.

Since the Jews have rejected Jesus as their true Messiah, (Savior) Romans 11:7-8 says, *"God has caused them to have a spirit of slumber."* In other words, they are spiritually, asleep while God's Spirit of Grace is spread abroad to the Gentiles. Israel needs to be awakened so they can see and understand that their true Messiah is Jesus Christ, and they can still accept Him even now, just as we can by simply believing in Him as our personal Savior.

This presentation of the Awesome Untold Story is divided into two parts

PART ONE

The first 3 ½ years of the 7 years of tribulation is not the wrath of God but the wrath of the antichrist poured out on all who oppose his New World Order. The New World Order is an evil world system designed to destroy all opposition, and ultimately exalt Satan through his right hand man, the antichrist, as king of all kingdoms of this world. He will be a counterfeit to Jesus Christ, "King of Kings, and Lord of Lords."

The antichrist mostly wants to destroy the 144,000 Jews mentioned in Rev. Ch.7. There are 12,000 from each of the 12 tribes. What is so special about these 144,000 Jews is that they have no Gentile blood mixed into them through intermarriage. They legally represent the nation of Israel in this war between God and Satan. If Satan can destroy them, then God cannot fulfill His promises to His chosen people. That would make God a liar on the same level as Satan, and God would no longer be able to legally cast Satan into the lake of fire. The lake of fire is Satan's worst fear. So, part one is about Satan trying to bring God down to his level by thwarting God's promises to His chosen people.

PART TWO

The second 3 ½ years of the great tribulation will be God pouring out His wrath on the kingdoms of the antichrist, and on the unrepentant reprobates who have rebelled against God, and harmed, or destroyed His people throughout history. God will systematically disassemble the one world order that the antichrist has set up during the first 3 ½ years.

Although the 144,000 Jews will be present on earth the entire 7 years of the tribulation, the Gentile believers will be removed from harms way via the rapture before God's wrath begins in the second 3 ½ years of tribulation. The 144,000 Jews will be hidden and protected from the antichrist during the second 3 ½ years of tribulation. At the end of the 7 years of tribulation will be the battle of Armageddon when Jesus will return with His saints to rescue the Jews who were hiding from the antichrist during the last 3 ½ years.

After the battle of Armageddon Jesus will establish a peaceful earthly kingdom where He will rule and reign with His saints for 1000 years. Satan will be bound during that time; however Satan will be released for a short time at the end of the 1000 years.

The 1000 year millennial reign of Christ will be followed by a final judgment which is called "The Great White Throne Judgment", and then a New Heaven, New Earth, and a New Jerusalem where believing saints (as the bride of Christ) will live forever.

This book is designed to study all chapters that pertain to the first 3 ½ years of tribulation when the antichrist is active, and then all chapters pertaining to the second 3 ½ years of tribulation when God takes revenge on the wicked.

The idea of doing it this way is to offer a better understanding of the sequence of events, and to better define the difference between the tribulation of the people of God in the first 3 ½ years, and the undiluted wrath of God against the antichrist and his people in the second 3 ½ years. The book of Revelation is **not** designed to scare us, but to prepare us for the things that will happen in the end times.

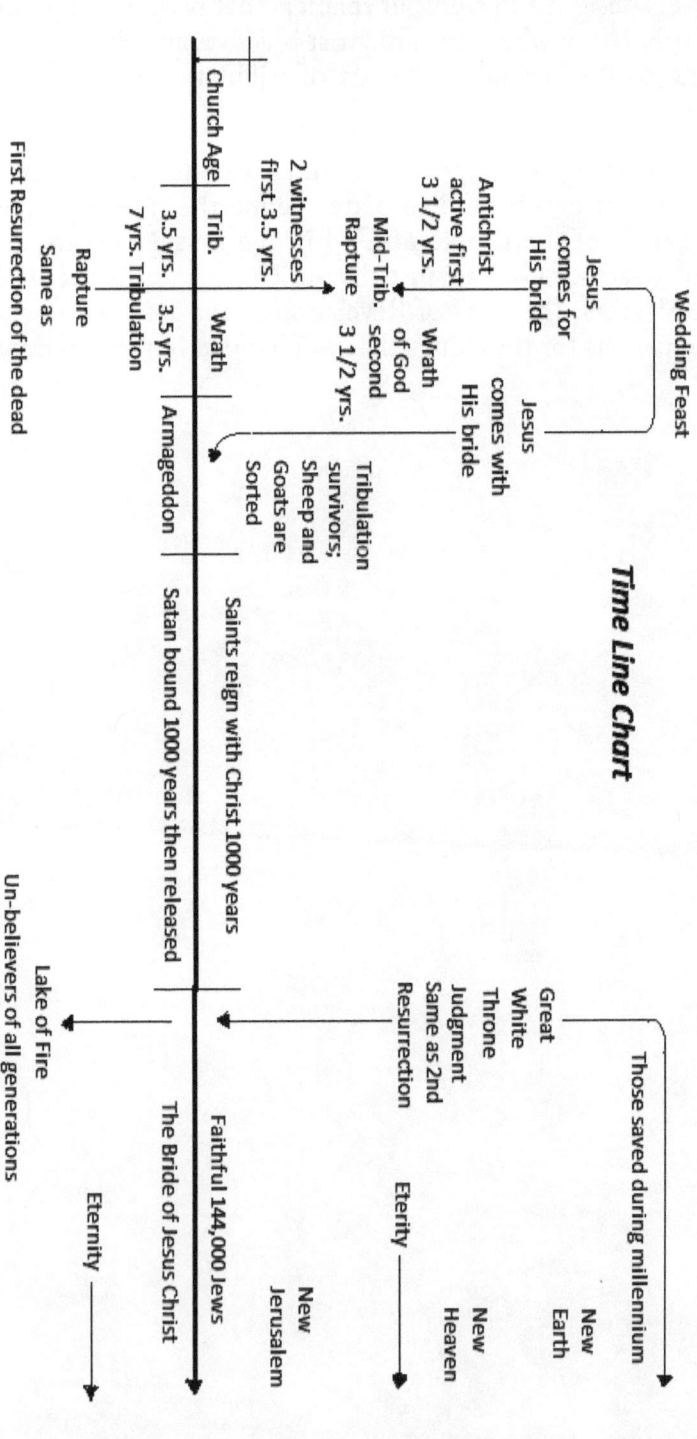

Book of Revelation
A Brief Overview

All believers know that God is Good, Holy, Righteous, True, and perfect in all His ways.

But God has an enemy called Satan who is just the opposite, and there is no good in him at all. He is out to steal God's creation from Him so that he can have all the glory for himself.

The book of Revelation is about a major war between God and Satan. God is out to save as many people as possible, especially His chosen people, the Jews. But Satan is out to destroy God's chosen people. But why are the Jews God's chosen people?

The Jews are **not** God's chosen people because they are righteous or faithful, but because God chose their blood line, beginning with faithful Abraham, to bring the Messiah, or Savior into the world. That Savior is Jesus Christ. Abraham was a man of pagan descent who believed God. God counted his faith for righteousness, and made great promises concerning his offspring. **Gen.12:3** *God said: I will bless them that bless thee, curse them that curse thee: and in thee shall all families of the earth be blessed.*

Jesus did come to earth through the blood line of the Jews as a baby in a stable at Bethlehem. He grew up and lived a perfect sinless life, and He preached about the kingdom of God. He tried to save as many people as possible. All they needed to do to be saved was to repent of their sins, and believe in Jesus; that He is their Messiah.

But when He came to deliver them from sin and oppression, and to set up His Kingdom on earth, they did not recognize Him as their

Messiah, because they were looking for a military leader to deliver them. So they demanded that He be crucified as an imposter.

He was rejected by the Jews, and crucified by the Roman soldiers, dead and buried, but since Jesus is God the Son, He has the power to lay His life down, and take it up again. On the third day He arose from the dead, and He ascended back to heaven.

Now the Jews are still waiting for their Messiah to come, and deliver them from sin and oppression. When actually He has already been here and they rejected Him.

Because they rejected Him, Romans 11: 7-8 says *"God has caused them to have a spirit of slumber"*, in other words, they are spiritually asleep, while God's Spirit of Grace is spread abroad to the Gentiles. Israel needs to be awakened so they can see and understand that their real Messiah is Jesus, and they can still accept Him even now, just as we can by simply repenting of our sins, and believing in Him as our personal Savior.

So God is still trying to win the Jews back to Him even though they have rejected Him. God will never ever give up on His chosen people. But the Jews are a stubborn, stiff necked people. They won't wake up without a major event happening to them.

That major event is called the great tribulation. It is a seven year period of time when terrible things will happen on this earth. All of these terrible events are designed to awaken the Jews, and to punish the people who have hated God and tried to destroy His people. So the book of Revelation is about the war that is taking place between God and Satan. (Good and evil)

God will try to awaken the Jews and win them to His side, while Satan just wants to destroy Jews and Christians so that God's promises cannot be fulfilled, and God becomes a liar like Satan is. God's main promise to the Jewish people in the Old Testament is, Ezekiel 37: 27-28 *someday God's tabernacle shall be with them and He will be their God and they shall be His people*. But that isn't happening right now, because they have rejected their Messiah.

Since the Jews have rejected Jesus as their Messiah they are still waiting for a Messiah to come to them, and that is a great opportunity for Satan to send a false messiah to deceive them. That false messiah will be the antichrist.

The antichrist will foster a seven year peace treaty with the Jews that will guarantee the Jews protection so they can build their long awaited temple, and begin sacrificing under the Mosaic Law. But in the middle of those seven years, as soon as they finish building their temple in Jerusalem, he will break the treaty, and try to destroy them. *Dan. 9:27*

The antichrist forces will hijack the newly built temple, and sit in the temple proclaiming himself to be God (II Thess.2: 4). At that time the Jews will wake up from their spiritual slumber and realize the antichrist is a deceiver, and Jesus is their true Messiah.

The Jews will then flee for their lives and scatter to get away from the antichrist and his armed forces. Satan will spend the rest of his time and energy trying to locate and destroy the Jewish people. Satan will go to any extreme to thwart God's plans for Israel.

Yes, Satan is that evil, and it is that important to him to destroy the Jews, and make God a liar. Believers know that Satan could never make God a liar but it's Satan's only hope of avoiding God's judgment for him which is the lake of fire where he will be tormented day and night forever Rev.20:10. The "lake of fire" is Satan's worst fear.

But God will somehow protect the Jews from the antichrist even while they are scattered. *Rev. 12:13-14*. God will also protect us: not so much from the troubles of that time because the antichrist will even target us as Christians, but God will not subject us to the anger that He will bring on those who are trying to harm His people. **How will He protect us?**

He will be with believers during these times of trouble which are mainly the first 3 ½ years. Then when the antichrist breaks the peace treaty with the Jews in the middle of the 7 years and tries to destroy them, God will intervene and call His people out of the world to be with Him: not only the living, but also those faithful people who have passed on before His return. I Thess.4:16, 17

He will rapture (rescue them) and change their mortal bodies into spiritual bodies that will never die, and we will forever be with the Lord. I Corin.15: 51-55. This is referring to the rapture; when Jesus takes His faithful people out of harms way.

Then God will proceed to pour out His undiluted wrath on the wicked people of the earth who have blasphemed His name. Blasphemy means to knowingly reject God, even with cursing.

So the last 3 ½ years of tribulation will be far worse than the first 3 ½, but believers won't be here for the last 3 ½ years because we will be with the Lord.

At the end of the 7 years of tribulation there will be a final battle called Armageddon which God will win, of course.

Then Satan will be subdued, and Jesus will set up His kingdom on earth which is called the millennium. The millennium is 1000 years of peace and tranquility. Everyone will get along just fine because Satan will be bound, and can't bother anyone.

After the 1000 years Satan will be released for a short time. Again he will try to rally multi-national forces to attack Israel; but God will defeat them and throw him into the lake of fire where he will be tormented day and night forever. *Rev.20:10*

But God's people will forever be with Him in a wonderful place called Heaven, the New Jerusalem, or the City that is Built Four Square.

The question is: When will all this take place?

No one except God knows exactly when, but there are signs of the times that tell us it could be soon, even within our life time.

Here are some things that might happen as we get closer to the days of tribulation.

There will be many imposters pretending to be Christ.

There will be wars, starvation, and disease in many more places of the world.

There will be higher than ever before crime waves, and the love of many will grow cold.

One might say these things are already happening, and to some extent that is true, but these last days events will be far worse than anything we are currently experiencing.

The antichrist will rise in power, and seem like a good person. He will have lots of good ideas for these times of trouble. He will be a powerful world statesman, and make a peace treaty with the Jews for 7 years. Then he will break the treaty, and try to destroy the Jews.

Someone will try to assassinate the antichrist, but when it looks like he is dead he will survive a terrible head wound, and people will think he is "supernatural."

After he survives the assassination attempt, possibly by an overly zealous so called Christian, he will begin to persecute the saints of God. Many of the lukewarm church people will be so afraid of him that they will betray true believers in their own churches and turn them over to the antichrist forces. This is a time of *apostasy* (Falling away from their faith).

Two witnesses from God begin to stand against the antichrist from the streets of Jerusalem and they continue for 3 ½ years. They will preach the truth of God. Many people will be torn as to whom to believe, the antichrist "answer man" or these two powerful men of God.

The antichrist wants to kill them but so many people worldwide are watching them and listening to them, that he cannot do it. Finally at the end of the 3 ½ years he does kill them, and their dead bodies lie on the streets of Jerusalem for 3 ½ days while most of the world celebrates their death. On the fourth day a loud voice from heaven says "COME UP HERE", and they are taken up to be with the Lord.

During the first 3 ½ years when the two witnesses were preaching…

A **false prophet** comes on the scene, and gives credibility to the antichrist who is now referred to as the beast because he often curses and blasphemes God, and even claims to be God. The title "beast" does not refer to his appearance, but to his character.

The **false prophet** calls on the people to make an image to the beast, and they make one.

The image of the beast will be an inanimate object; probably the most powerful and sophisticated computer ever built in the image of a man. It will be a very charismatic, pre-programmed talking head.

The **false prophet** has power to give the appearance of life to the image of the beast so that it can both speak, and cause all those who will **not** worship the beast or take his mark, to be killed.

The antichrist will try to make everyone take an invisible mark, such as a bar code, or computer chip in their right hand or forehead, and without it they cannot buy or sell.

This mark can be used to keep track of people whom the antichrist wants to control, or sort out for destruction such as criminals, Jews, or Christians.

Many will take the mark voluntarily but most true Christians will refuse to, and they will be labeled enemies of the state (or enemies of humanity) and will be killed for refusing.

Rev.14: 9-10 says *"If any man worship the beast and his image and receives his mark in his forehead, or in his hand, The same shall drink of the wine of the wrath of God, which is poured out without mixture into the cup of His indignation; and he shall be tormented with fire and brimstone in the presence of the holy angels, and in the presence of the Lamb."*

Under no circumstances should a believer willingly take the mark of the beast.

Although the children of God will undergo tribulation during the first 3 ½ years, they will never undergo the wrath of God. *(Rom.5: 9, and 1 Thess. 5: 9)* As believers we are at peace with God.

God will get all of His people out of harms way, via the rapture, before the second 3 ½ years of great tribulation begins. He will then pour out His undiluted wrath on the wicked people who are *left behind.*

Due to the first 3 ½ years of tribulation, the broken treaty by the antichrist, and the powerful testimony of the two witnesses, the Jews will be awakened from their spiritual slumber, and they will know that Jesus is their true Messiah. They will once again be His people, and He will be their God just as He promised.

So the reason Jesus inspired the apostle John to write the book of Revelation on the island of Patmos is to warn, prepare, protect, encourage, and fortify believers for what they will experience in the end times when the antichrist becomes active.

The book of Revelation is **not** designed to scare us, but to prepare us for things that shall shortly come to pass.

DANIEL Chapter 9

The 70th week of Daniel

A week of years

If you're ever looking in the Bible for an example of a person of prayer; Daniel might be the first name that comes to mind. Daniel loved to communicate with the Lord in prayer.

Dan.9: 20-23 (paraphrased) while Daniel was praying, the angel Gabriel touched him and said, *"Daniel, you are greatly loved, therefore understand the vision I have given you."*

Q. To what other important person, or persons in scripture, did the angel Gabriel appear?

A. Mary; the mother of Jesus, and Zacharias the priest, and father of John the Baptist.

This is the prophecy given to Daniel by the angel Gabriel: **Dan.9: 24** *Seventy weeks are determined upon the Jewish people, to finish the transgression, to make an end to their sins, to make reconciliation for iniquity,* (make restitution for past sins). In other words, a dead line of 70 weeks is given for Israel to clean up their act, and **to recognize their Messiah.**

One might ask: how could the Jewish people recognize their Messiah within the next 70 weeks when we know Jesus will not come to them for hundreds of years from the time of Daniel? Here's what the scholars and commentators tell us.

The definition of one "week" is, 7 parts of time. (a week of days, months, years, etc.).

Q. A week of days would be how long?   Answer. 7 days.

Q. A week of years would be how long?   Answer. 7 years.

The general belief of most commentaries is 70 weeks equals Seventy weeks of years.

If that is true then seventy x Seven (One week of years) = 490 years of punishment on the Jewish people; most likely for ignoring the Sabbath day of rest and worship for 490 years.

Lev.26: 34-35 says this: *Then shall the land enjoy her Sabbaths, as long as it lies desolate, and you be in your enemies' land; even then shall the land rest, and enjoy her Sabbaths. As long as it lies desolate it shall rest; because it did not rest in your Sabbaths, when you dwelt upon it.*

Like people, even land needs time to rest and rejuvenate. Otherwise it becomes depleted. So, Israel has 70 weeks of years (490yrs.) *to make an end to sin, and bring in everlasting righteousness;* in other words; to recognize their Messiah, when He comes.

Dan.9: 25 tells us that *from the time the decree went forth to rebuild Jerusalem unto the Messiah* (Jesus) *totals 69 weeks of years.* (7+60+2=69) The Jewish Messiah came more than 2000 years ago, so 69 of those 70 weeks have already been accomplished. Then apparently God put the 70th week on hold. He hits the pause button so to speak. Why: to allow the Gentiles an opportunity to believe on Jesus and be saved?

Seventy weeks minus 69 before the cross, leaves one week of years, or 7 years left over. The pause time between the 69th and 70th week is the church age; the age of grace when God reaches out to the Gentiles, because the Jewish people rejected Jesus as their Messiah.

The age of grace is based on **John 3: 16.** *For God so loved the world, that He gave His only begotten Son, that* **whosoever** (Jew or Gentile) *believeth on Him should not perish, but have ever lasting life.* The age of grace is now over 2000 years down range. God hit the pause button, so to speak, when the Jewish Messiah was cut off. (Crucified)

Most likely God will restart the clock for the 70th week when the 7 year peace treaty with the Jews is fostered and signed by the antichrist. *Daniel 9:27a*

Daniel 9: 27a: *and he* (antichrist) *shall confirm the covenant (treaty) with many for one week* (7 years). So this is probably when the clock will start for the 70th week of Daniel; also known as the 7 years of tribulation.

The church age, in which we are living, will end with the fullness of the Gentiles; when the last Gentile who should be saved, is saved; just before believers are gathered unto the Lord. *Romans 11:25*

Romans 11: 25 *I would not brethren that ye be ignorant of this mystery, lest ye be wise in your own conceit; that <u>blindness in part is happened to Israel,</u> **until** <u>the fullness of the Gentiles be come in.</u>*

At that time; near the middle of the 7 year treaty, the 144,000 Jews will recognize Jesus as their Messiah.

~~~~~~

Another thing that should be noted in the book of Daniel is in chapter 12 and verse 4.

Daniel 12: 4 *O Daniel, shut up the words, and seal the book, even to the time of the end: many shall run to and fro, and knowledge shall be increased.*

It's easy to see that Daniel's prophecy is our reality. We are living in a time of modern methods of transportation, and state of the art technical advancements, and yet these are perilous times of uncertainty and rapid change.

~ Part One ~

First 3 ½ Years of Seven Year Tribulation

REVELATION Chapter 1

John commissioned to write to 7 churches

Rev.1: 1-3 This is **not** the revelation of John, but the revelation of Jesus Christ for John to write about things that must shortly come to pass. **Verse 3** says *there is a special blessing for those who read and hear the words of this prophecy: **if** they retain what they hear; for the time is at hand.* What does that mean? It means that every generation should be prepared for the possibility of end time events.

Rev.1: 7 is a good example of why we **can't** always study Revelation verse by verse. Revelation is not written in chronological order. We are studying the letters to the 7 churches, but verse 7 speaks of the return of Christ. So we need to set verse 7 aside for now, and pick it up later when we get to that subject. We're not skipping verse 7 but setting it aside.

Rev.1: 9 John was exiled to the island of Patmos by the Roman Government due to *testifying of the word of God, and his testimony of Jesus Christ*. John is suffering and feeling the effects of persecution himself.

Rev.1: 10, 11 *John was in the Spirit on the Lord's Day*, (he was worshiping on the Sabbath day). The glorified Jesus appears to the apostle John and tells him to write to the seven churches in Asia Minor (Modern day Turkey).

These letters were designed to evaluate their spiritual condition, and to warn and prepare them for the future events that were to come. These 7 churches might represent all churches of all ages, (Seven being the biblical number for completeness).

Rev.1: 12-19 when John saw the glorified risen Savior, he fell or fainted at His feet. Jesus touched him and kindly said *"Fear not, I am the first and the last. Write what you have seen."*

Rev.1: 18 Jesus says *"I have the keys of death and hell."* Before the crucifixion Satan had the keys of death and hell. So how did Jesus take the keys away from him?

Matt.12: 40 says: after the crucifixion, *Jesus descended to the heart of the earth for three days.* Jesus legally took possession of the keys of death and hell. Because He is sinless, Satan had no authority to keep Him there.

People who died before the resurrection of Christ went to Sheol (the place of departed spirits) located in the heart of the earth. They either went to the tormented side called Hades, or to the comforted side called the bosom of Abraham.

Luke 16: 19-22, *a certain rich man, which was clothed in purple and fine linen, and fared sumptuously every day: and there was a certain beggar named Lazarus, which was laid at his gate, full of sores. And desiring to be fed with the crumbs which fell from the rich man's table: more over the dogs licked his sores. The beggar died and was carried by the angels into Abraham's bosom: the rich man also died and was buried.*

Notice that the dogs did a better job of ministering to Lazarus than the rich man did. They at least licked his sores and kept them somewhat clean. Lazarus died and was escorted by angels to the comforted side of Sheol; also known as Abraham's bosom. The rich man also died. Now let's hear what happened to him in Hades.

Luke 16: 23-26 *in hell he lift up his eyes, being in torments, and seeth Abraham a far off, and Lazarus in his bosom. And he cried and said, Father Abraham, have mercy on me, and send Lazarus, that he may dip the tip of his finger in water, and cool my tongue: for I am tormented in this flame.*

Notice that in hell the rich man can see Lazarus in Abraham's bosom on the other side of a great gulf. The rich man in torment begs for mercy. He still sees Lazarus as an inferior and asks Abraham to send him over with a little bit of water to relieve his suffering.

What did the rich man do when Lazarus was suffering? He did absolutely nothing.

But Abraham informs him of the great divide that cannot be crossed between the tormented side, and the comforted side of Sheol.

We know all this happened before the cross because Jesus is telling this story. So what happened after Jesus was crucified and descended to the heart of the earth, and took the keys of death and hell away from Satan?

Then He preached the good news (the death, burial, and resurrection) to the captives on the comforted side of Sheol. **Who are the captives?**

Eph.4: 8-10 *when He ascended up on high, he led captivity captive, and gave gifts unto men. Now that He ascended what is it but that He also descended first into the lower parts of the earth? He that descended is the same also that ascended up far above all things.*

The good news was that when He ascended, those faithful people who died before the cross could rise with Him on the third day. So He led the captives out of Sheol into heaven.

After the resurrection, Hades did **not** change places, it's still in the heart of the earth, but the comforted side is now paradise raised (which is called heaven). Now when believers die they are *absent from the body, and present with the Lord* in heaven. *II Corin.5:8* The resurrection of Jesus Christ made that possible.

REVELATION Chapter 2
Letters to Churches

In **Rev. Ch.2-3** The Glorified Jesus dictates to the apostle John on the island of Patmos letters of evaluation of the 7 churches of Asia Minor, which is modern day western Turkey.

The 7 churches are: Ephesus, Smyrna, Pergamos, Thyatira, Sardis, Philadelphia, and Laodicea.

The two churches of the 7 that have no stated problems are Smyrna and Philadelphia. The two churches that receive no praise are Sardis and Laodicea. The churches of today could learn a lot from what was said to each of these 7 churches.

Rev.2: 1 unto the angel of the church of Ephesus John is told to write these things.

John's letter is not written to an actual angel, but to the human minister of the church of Ephesus. John refers to the human minister as an angel, because he is a ministering spirit.

Heb.1: 7 KJV tells us that the word angel means "ministering spirit." All pastors are ministering spirits so that's why John calls the pastors of these churches "angels." They too are ministering spirits.

Rev.2: 2-4 Jesus says, *"I know your works, patience, your distain of evil, your discernment of false teachers."* Wow, they're off to a good start. *Nevertheless, the problem is you have left your first love.* They were losing enthusiasm for the Lord.

Rev.2: 5 -7 the prescription is: Remember from where you have fallen, Repent and Return to your first works. We must not take our faith for granted, or become complacent like this church in Ephesus.

Then the promise to the over comers is that they may eat of the tree of life which is in the midst of the paradise of God. That's quite a promise.

Remember access to the tree of life was denied to Adam and Eve after their fall lest they eat and live forever in their fallen state. Gen.3:22 But we will have full access to that tree.

Rev.2: 8-9 unto the angel (human minister) of the church of Smyrna write;

"I know your works, tribulation, and your poverty, but you are rich."

Rev.2: 10 Smyrna was a suffering church. They suffered persecution, poverty, blasphemy, imprisonment, and death. But their reward was a crown of life.

Some of these faithful saints were imprisoned 10 days, and then killed. What is the significance of the 10 days? One must wonder if 10 days is how long the antichrist will give believers to comply with a state mandate to accept the mark of the beast, or be beheaded. Beheading will be the weapon of choice the antichrist will use against his enemies. Rev.20: 4

Rev.2: 12-13 to the angel (human minister) of the church in Pergamos write…

I know your works, and that you dwell in Satan's territory, (they were experiencing extreme persecution), *but you have not denied me, even in the face of martyrdom.*

Rev.2: 14 I have a few things against you; you have among you those who hold to the doctrine of Balaam. Numbers 22-24 Balaam may have been a Jewish prophet who lived outside of Israel in Pethor, in the region of Mesopotamia east of Israel. Balaam had strong connections to the God of Abraham; but Balaam compromised his faith by receiving payment to seduce Israel into sin. (Such as immorality, and eating meat sacrificed to idols) Numbers 31:15, 16, Jude 1:11

Rev.2: 15-16 Some among you hold to false doctrine of the Nicolaitans. Repent or I will come quickly and fight against you with the sword of my mouth (Condemnation).

Rev.2: 18-19 unto the church in Thyatira write; says the Son of God, whose eyes are like a flame of fire and feet like fine brass Rev.1:14-15. I know your works, charity, service, and faith, and the last is more than the first." (Their faith out weighed their works).

Rev.2: 20-21 Nevertheless, you tolerated a "would be" prophetess (Jezebel) who caused Christians to stumble into immorality and defilement. God gave her time to repent, but she would not.

God will often give us time to repent. This woman **did not** repent, but the woman caught in adultery John Ch.8 did repent. She couldn't change her past, but she allowed Jesus to change her future.

Rev.2: 22-23 reads that the Lord will throw her, and her fellow sinners, into a bed of great tribulation, and kill her children. Read Exodus 34:6-7 Not necessarily kill her children physically, but when one generation doesn't teach the next about the Lord they are putting them at great risk, spiritually, and every other way. And that generation will put the next generation at risk.

Rev.2: 24-27 implies: those who overcome and remain faithful, will be given power to rule the nations during the millennial reign of Christ. They will be given positions of authority throughout the world. We will un-pack this in Ch.20 when we study the millennium.

REVELATION Chapter 3

Letters to the Churches

Rev.3: 1 *Unto the angel (human minister) of the church in* **Sardis** *write; says (Jesus) who has the seven spirits of God.*

The 7 spirits of God seem to represent the all-knowing, all seeing, Omni-presence of God.

"I know your works, your church has a reputation of being alive, but you are dead." Wow, the whole town thinks this church is alive and well, but they are dead. That's sad.

When is a church dead? A church is dead when the Holy Spirit has little or no effect on all, or nearly all of the congregation.

Rev.3: 2 *Strengthen what remains before it also dies. James 4: 8 says: draw nigh unto the Lord, and He will draw nigh unto you.* This church in Sardis is almost dead but;

Isaiah 42:3 says: a bruised reed he shall not break, smoking flax he shall not quench. No matter how weak they are in their faith, or how emotionally damaged they are, if they sincerely ask him; Jesus will restore them. He'll bind up that bruised reed until it's healed. He will fan that smoldering ember until it's a flame of faith. That's just the kindness of the Lord. His prescription for the church of Sardis is in verse 3.

Rev.3: 3 ***Remember*** *how you first received Jesus;* ***hold fast*** *to that and* ***repent*** *before it's too late.*

Rev.3: 4 there are a few in Sardis who have **not** defiled themselves, they have remained faithful. Isn't that the way it always is? There's always a faithful few in every church, and they are the ones who do most of the work.

Rev.3: 5-6 Over comers shall be clothed in white. (White robes represent righteousness)

Rev.3: 7-8 unto the angel (human minister) of the church of **Philadelphia** write: *"I know your works; I have set before you an open door."* Philadelphia was a good church.

What is this open door? It is "Freedom in Christ." *John 10: 9* Jesus said *"I am the door: by me if any man enters in, he shall be saved, and shall go in and out, and find pasture.*

Even when this church at Philadelphia was in a weakened state they did not deny Jesus or His word.

Rev.3: 10 KJV, *"Because you have kept my word of patience,"* Jesus says *"I will keep you from the hour of temptation, which shall come upon all the world"*

KJV, Jesus did **not** say, "I will keep you from *tribulation*, but from *temptation*." Some versions say **trials**. The question is; what are these temptations and trials.

Speaking of the end times *Matt.24:24* says: *many false Christ and false prophets shall show great signs and wonders; insomuch that, if it were possible, they shall deceive even the very elect.* (God's people)

Jesus will keep us from the **temptation** to believe that these false prophets and their signs and wonders are for real. He will also keep us from being **tempted** to take the mark of the beast even under severe pressure and persecution.

Jesus does **not** say in *Ch.3:10* that He will keep us from **tribulation** as some would have us think. They use this verse to argue for a pre-tribulation rapture by sighting this as proof that we will be raptured before the 7 years of tribulation begins.

Jesus said *"In this world you will have tribulation, but be of good cheer, I have overcome the world." John 16: 33*

Christians are not immune to tribulation, temptation or trials. By the grace of God we can overcome them. **We are immune to the wrath of God,** because we are at peace with God.

Rev.3: 14 unto the angel (human minister) of the church of **Laodicea** write…

Says (Jesus), the faithful and true witness, the beginning of the creation of God.

Jesus was physically created in the flesh, but this isn't talking about His 33 years on earth. It's talking about the beginning of creation.

Contrary to the Jehovah Witness's interpretation of this verse, it's not saying that Jesus is the beginning of the **created** of God. Jesus is **not created**, He is the **creator.**

John 1: 1-3 says: *in the beginning was the Word, and the Word was with God, and the Word was God. The same was in the beginning with God. All things were made by Him; and without Him was not anything made that was made.* Jesus who is the same yesterday, today and forever spoke all things into existence.

Colossians 1: 14-17 *In whom we have redemption through His blood, even the forgiveness of sins: Who is the image of the invisible God, the firstborn of every creature: For by Him were all things created, that are in heaven, and that are in earth, visible and invisible, whether they be thrones, or dominions, or principalities, or powers: all things were created by Him, and for Him:*

When Rev.3: 14 says Jesus is the beginning of the creation of God, it means that Jesus was the creator from the very beginning of creation; **not** that He was created by God.

Rev.3: 15-16 *"I know your works that you are neither cold nor hot, I wish you were one or the other! So because you are lukewarm – neither hot or cold, I will spit you out of my mouth."* Luke warm means spiritually uncommitted, undecided, or double minded. *Matt.12: 30* Jesus said, *"He that is not with me is against me."*

Rev.3: 17 you say *"you are rich and need nothing."* This lukewarm church at Laodicea trusted so much in their riches that they were blind to their wretchedness. Their priorities were out of order.

Rev.3: 19 all that God loves He chastens, but He doesn't want to chasten us. Therefore, Jesus says, "Repent."

Rev.3: 20 *I stand at the door* (of your heart) *and knock: **if anyone** hears my voice, and opens the door, **I will come in** and eat* (commune) *with him, and he with me.* We must open the door of our heart; Jesus will **not** come in uninvited.

From *verse 18 to 22* Jesus does nothing but **woo** the church of **Laodicea** to repent, and trust Him to cover their sins.

REVELATION Chapter 4
John's Vision of Heaven

Rev.4: 1 After this John says, *"I saw an open door in heaven."*

After John wrote the 7 letters to the ministers of the 7 churches in Asia Minor

A voice says **to John,** *"**Come up here** and I will show **you** things to come."* Many people think that "Come Up Here" is the Pre-tribulation rapture of all believers. *In my opinion* it's **not** likely that "Come up here" has anything to do with the rapture. The voice calls **John** up for an expressed purpose, and that is to see, and to write about things to come.

Rev.4: 2 immediately, **"I"** was in the Spirit. The voice spoke specifically to **John.** So, "Come up here" has nothing to do with the pre-tribulation rapture. If it did the rapture would have happen 2000 years ago, when John was called up, and we would have missed it.

Some people say *the church* (the body of Christ) is never mentioned again in the book of Revelation after chapter 4, therefore the rapture must have happened before the 7 years of tribulation begins, but that is **not** true. The church is mentioned in at least 10 different ways after Ch.4 such as: *"**brethren** Rev.6:11, **chosen,** Rev.17:14, **faithful** Rev. 17:14, **fellow servants,** Rev. 6:11, **martyrs** Rev.17:6, **over comers** Rev. 21:7, **priests of God** Rev.20:6, **prophets** Rev.16:6, **saints** Rev.13:7, **witnesses** Rev. 20:4, **them that keep the sayings of this book** Rev.22:9, **believers**, and more."*

Some say, "The rapture is the next thing on God's calendar of events." In my opinion that is not true. There are several more things that must happen before the rapture will occur.

II Thess.2: 1-4 tells us that *before Jesus gathers believers to himself, there shall come a falling away* (from the faith), *and the man of sin* (antichrist) *must be revealed, who opposes and exalts himself above all that is called God, and he must sit in the temple of God* (not yet built in Jerusalem) *showing himself as God.*

II Thess.2: 6-8 says: *And now we know what withholds that he* (antichrist) *might be revealed in his time. For the* **mystery of iniquity** *doth already work: only* **he** (Holy Spirit) *who now lets (allows), will let until* **he** *be taken out of the way.*

The H.S. is withholding the antichrist from being revealed. The **"what"** in verse 6 is the church, and the **"he"** in verse 7 is the Holy Spirit. So the church and the Holy Spirit <u>must co-operate</u> to restrain evil. In these verses 6-8 the term "mystery of iniquity" seems to imply that as more and more people refrain from practicing faith in Jesus Christ, the *power* of the Holy Spirit will be more and more withdrawn until the Wicked One can actually be revealed.

Please remember: **the *Holy Spirit cannot be completely taken out of the way because He is Omni-present*.** However the *restraining power* of the Holy Spirit will be continuously withdrawn at that time of apostasy. When enough restraining power is withdrawn the antichrist will be revealed, and the rapture will occur sometime after that.

Also, the persecution of the saints, by the antichrist, must occur before Jesus gathers believers unto Himself. **Rev.13: 7** says: *"And it was given unto him (antichrist) to make war with the saints, and to overcome them: and power was given him over all kindred, and tongues, and nations."* The saints will have to be present on earth at the same time the antichrist is for the antichrist to make war with them, and to martyr them. So the rapture cannot precede the revealing of the antichrist.

Rev.4: 3 without going into detail, it suffices to say; He that sat upon the throne was magnificent, majestic, and awesome.

Rev.4: 4 *around the throne sat 24 elders clothed in white with gold crowns.* Who are the 24 elders? Probably twelve were from the Old Testament, and twelve from the New Testament. (OT, 12 sons of Jacob, which became the twelve tribes of Israel, and the NT, 12 disciples of Jesus; Judas was replaced)

Rev. 4: 6-9 *there were four beasts full of eyes.* Who are these four heavenly beings? The word beast can mean heavenly being, or heavy load bearer.

Four things I noticed about these 4 heavenly beings: 1. they had 6 wings, 2. they did fly, 3. they cried Holy, Holy, Holy, and 4. they gave glory to God.

Let's go to *Isaiah 6: 2-3* and we will discover exactly who these 4 heavenly beings are.

Isaiah 6: 2-3 *above it* (The throne of God) *stood the Seraphim: each one had* **six wings**; *with twain he covered his face, and with twain he covered his feet, and with twain he* **did fly**. *And one cried unto another, and said,* **Holy, holy, holy,** *earth is full of* **his glory**. These 4 heavenly beings are 4 Seraphim angels.

Cherubim angels are innumerable, they seem to be like the worker bees, but Seraphim are seldom mentioned in scripture. They seem to be the more elite angels, very powerful, but fewer in numbers, and always close to the throne of God.

Rev. 4: 10-11 The 24 elders fell down and worshiped saying, *"Thou art worthy O Lord, for you have created all things and for your pleasure they were created."*

All things were created for God's pleasure, including you and me. So why are we on this earth; ***to please God?*** It pleased God to put us here, and now that we're here we need to please Him. How do we do that? We do it through worship and obedience.

Mark 12: 30-31 Love *the Lord thy God with all your heart, soul, mind, and strength, and love your neighbor as yourself.* It finishes up by saying there is no other commandment greater than these. This is pleasing to God.

REVELATION Chapter 5
The Book with 7 Seals

Rev.5: 1 The book (scroll) in the right hand of God the Father is a legal document so it is sealed. This book could be the **title deed to the earth**, which Satan illegitimately tricked Adam into turning over to him in the Garden of Eden. Satan is a legalist, so in his opinion it is legal, but in God's opinion it was trickery and deceit.

Adam being the only person on earth in the beginning was given ownership of the earth; under the one condition that he **not** partake of the tree of the knowledge of good and evil.

Adam relinquished his ownership by rebelling against God, and obeying Satan. Satan became his new master. Adam became Satan's slave, and everything Adam owned became Satan's including this world.

II Corin.4: 4 Satan is called *the god of this world who has blinded the minds of them who believe not.* Through deception Satan claims ownership of this world, but God is in control, and He will legally take it back through redemption. (Redemption means to redeem or reclaim)

Rev.5: 2-4 the question is asked, *"Who is worthy to open this book and loose the seven seals? …………..John wept much because no man was found worthy to open this book.* Why was John so upset that no one was worthy in heaven or earth to open this book?

John walked and talked with Jesus, he saw the miracles, the sick, blind, and lame were healed, the dead raised to life; he saw Jesus walk on water, and he saw His ascension from the Mt. of Olives into heaven. He must have wondered, how could Jesus **not** be worthy? And if He's not worthy then no-one is. If no-one is then this "Jesus thing" was all a big scam. Why wouldn't John be upset?

Rev.5: 5-6 an elder said to John, *"Weep not; the Lion of Judah has prevailed to open the book, and to loose the 7 seals."*

John saw in the midst of the throne, and the 4 beasts, and the 24 elders, a Lamb stood as it had been slain.

Last chapter we determined that the 4 beasts were, **what?** Four Seraphim angels *(Isaiah 6:2-3)* and the 24 elders were, **who?** (12 sons of Jacob of the OT, and 12 disciples of the NT)

Amazingly, John would have actually seen himself as one of those 24 elders in this prophetic vision of the future.

Rev.5:7 *The Son takes the book (*that could be **the title deed to the earth**)*, from the Father's right hand.*

Rev.5:9 *they sung a new song. Thou art worthy to open the seals for you have redeemed us from every people, tongue, and nation.* Who are all these people who have been redeemed from the earth? Are they raptured believers? We cannot make that assumption.

Verse 9 In John's heavenly vision he is seeing a multitude of faithful Old Testament believers who are already in heaven **since** the resurrection of Jesus. They were formerly held in "Sheol". Before the cross, Sheol was the holding place of departed spirits.

This group also includes every New Testament believer who has ever died, and gone to heaven up to the time of John's vision. These people were **not** raptured when John was told to "Come up here". If they were, the rapture would have happened 2000 years ago and we would have missed it. So this first group is any faithful person who has ever died and gone to heaven up to the time of John's heavenly vision.

They are spiritually alive in the presence of the Lord; even though their bodies are still in graves. When Jesus descended, and then ascended from the lower parts of the earth (Sheol), He led these captives out of the place of departed spirits; before the cross, to what we now call heaven. Jesus death, burial, and resurrection made all this possible. *Eph.3: 8-10*

Rev.5: 11–14 *all of heaven burst out into praise and worship of the Lamb who is worthy to open the 7 seals.*

This is the first of three huge groups who will suddenly show up in heaven in John's heavenly vision. Only one of these three groups will be the raptured saints. This group is **not** the raptured saints. This first group mostly consists of faithful Old Testament believers.

REVELATION Chapter 6
Six of Seven Seals opened

The **First 3 ½ years** of the tribulation is not the wrath of God; it is the wrath of the antichrist against anyone who opposes his One World agenda.

In John's vision of heaven he sees the Lamb is about to open the scroll with 7 seals as He reclaims what could be **the Title deed to the earth**. It contains condemnation for the enemies of God, and a battle plan to take back the kingdoms of this world. *Rev.11:15b*

Rev.6: 1-2 In John's vision of heaven he sees the Lamb (Jesus) open the **first seal**. He sees *a **white horse** and the rider has a bow, and a crown. He goes out to conquer.*

A white horse could mean he appears to be a valiant leader, a bow could mean he does **not** appear to be very threatening; a crown could mean that he speaks with authority. His goal is to conquer people. Not necessarily to kill them but to control them. You don't have to kill people to conquer them. He is probably a very charismatic orator. Many say this rider is the antichrist, but I don't think so.

This rider on the white horse could be a powerful world statesman who will rapidly organize groups of countries to unite into kingdoms. There will be a total of 10 kingdoms worldwide. They will be ruled by the antichrist. This white horse rider could be a worldwide community organizer. Each of the 10 kingdoms will be composed of several counties. The antichrist will appoint over them 10 evil kings who are loyal to him.

The question is: how will the antichrist control such an enormous worldwide system as this? By controlling these ten kings, the antichrist will attempt to control the whole world. He will order the 10 kings to set up a data based marking system that will identify those who are for his One World Government system, and those who are against it. Those who are opposed will be dealt with individually. This worldwide community organizer, riding on a white horse, is followed by three even more hellish horsemen.

Rev.6: 3-4 Jesus opens the **Second seal, a Red horse;** *the rider was given power to take peace from the earth.* If he takes peace from the earth, ***what's left?*** There will be constant wars and rumors of wars. These are not big wars, or nuclear wars, but worldwide skirmishes.

People tend to fear rapid change. They will be concerned about what will happen if their countries are clustered into kingdoms, and how that might affect their borders, laws, freedoms, and national sovereignty. Many countries will violently resist these changes.

This red horse rider was given a *"great sword"*. This could mean that he will also be the chief enforcer against those who refuse to take the mark of the beast. People will be afraid of what will happen if they take the mark, because most faithful churches will preach that the Bible says not to receive the mark of the beast under any circumstances.

People will also be afraid of what will happen if they refuse to take the mark of the beast.

At first it will be optional because of its popularity, but soon it will become mandatory. People will be afraid **not** to take the mark because without it they cannot buy or sell. That is a big problem for people with families. *Rev.13:17*

Rev.6: 5-6 when the **Third seal** is opened, John sees a **Black horse;** *whose rider had a pair of balances in his hand* which could imply that this will be a time of shortages, or contrived shortages as in hoarding, or rationing of necessities (A time of desperation). Shortages, hoarding, and rationing are often the results of wars.

It's likely that the antichrist will emerge as a problem solver, and assure the world that not much will change as a result of their being included into one of the kingdoms of the world, and there might even be mutually shared benefits. This will make sense to most people, and they will settle down, and come on board. ***But the antichrist will have rapidly achieved his goal of establishing the 10 world kingdoms.***

Rev.6: 7-8 the **Fourth Seal** Jesus opens reveals a **Pale horse;** *the name of the rider was Death; and Hell followed him.*

The rider named *"Death"* could be the **antichrist**, and the one named *"Hell"* could be the **false prophet** spoken of in *Rev.13:11-12*.

Power was given to Death and Hell (By Satan of course) *to kill ¼ of the earth's population in four ways.*

1. **By sword** – by order of the antichrist, martyrs beheaded for refusing the mark of the beast *Rev.20: 4;* also by order of the antichrist many will die of hunger.
2. **Hunger** - because they cannot buy or sell without the mark. *Rev.13: 16-17*
3. **Plagues** – malnutrition can bring on various parasites, deceases, and pandemics.
4. **Beasts of the field** - we can only speculate as to how this might happen, but most of these people are killed, or allowed to die, for not taking the mark of the beast.

One forth of the world's population dead, but thankfully, they didn't take the mark of the beast. So most likely they will be martyred into the presence of the Lord.

Rev.6: 9 the **Fifth Seal** is opened; John saw *under the altar the souls of them who were slain for the word of God, and for their testimony.* These are faithful martyrs and overcomers, but why are they under the altar?

Their bodies are in graves, but their souls are in **close proximity** to God. Under the altar could imply that they are pleading for justice at the feet of God *Rev. 8:3*. Note: That the location of the golden altar is before the throne of God. It contains the prayers of all who have been wronged, but have trusted God to take vengeance on their enemies.

Rev.6: 10 they cried with a loud voice, *"How long Oh Lord, holy and true, do you not judge and avenge our blood on them that dwell on the earth?"*

Verse 10 Implies that, as of the fifth seal, the Lord has not yet begun to take revenge on the wicked people of the earth. His wrath has not yet begun.

Rev.6: 11 First things first, even before answering their question, *they were given white robes,* (which represent righteousness) *and then invited to enter into a heavenly rest.*

He asked them to relax, and to trust Him to deal with their enemies. Then He explained to them that ***more*** *of their fellow servants must be killed as they were* (Before He will intervene). Though millions are being martyred, millions are trusting in Jesus for their salvation.

This strongly implies that, as of the fifth seal, the rapture has not yet taken place, nor has the wrath of God. The antichrist is still making war with the saints for refusing to take the mark of the beast. *Rev.13:7*

So, the saints have to be present on earth during the first 3 ½ years of the tribulation. Why; because they are needed here to lead people to the Lord in these troubled times. It's likely that more people will be saved during the first 3 ½ years of the tribulation, than any other 3 ½ year period in the history of the world.

Rev.6: 12-14 when the **Sixth Seal** is opened; there will be a powerful ***worldwide earthquake*** *that moves every mountain and island out of its place. The sun, moon, and stars are darkened,* perhaps due to volcanic ash. An earthquake of this magnitude would trigger worldwide volcanic activity. It will also trigger worldwide tsunamis that will kill many people in shore line areas.

This earthquake, as horrible as it is, is a natural disaster. It is **not** the wrath of God. The actual wrath of God can**not** begin until all believers are out of harms way. Although believers are subject to tribulation, trials, temptations, and persecution they are **not** subject to the wrath of God. *Rom.5:9, Rom.8:1, I Thess.5:9*

I Thess.5: 9 For God has **not** appointed us to wrath, but to obtain salvation by our Lord Jesus Christ.

Rev.6: 15-17 at this time all levels of society will be aware of the outrage of God. Believers, who fear the Lord, will be thinking *"Even so, come, Lord Jesus"* while unbelievers, who don't really fear, or reverence God, will be terrified beyond measure, and hopelessly lost.

As of the sixth seal the rapture has **not** taken place in our study, nor has the wrath of God. There are only 7 seals. So, the 7th seal will be the wrath of God in the second 3 ½ years of the great tribulation.

REVELATION Chapter 7
The 144,000 SEALED

Rev.7: 1-2 *Four angels are standing on the four corners of the earth holding back the winds.* What winds: probably the windstorms of God's judgment? This implies that the wrath of God has not yet begun.

We know the earth is round, but the **four corners** of the earth could refer to the four corners of a compass; North, South, East, and West, the totality of the earth.

Rev.7: 3-8 *A fifth angel tells the first four angels **not** to hurt the earth or sea until the servants of God are sealed in their foreheads.* This mark may or may not be visible.

The total number of those who were sealed is 144,000. There were twelve thousand from each of the 12 tribes of Israel. Can we know what kind of a mark will be on their foreheads? The answer is yes. *Rev.14:1* tells us it will be the Father's name. In the Old Testament that name would be **Yahweh**.

The 144,000 Jews may, or may not know why they have been marked in their foreheads. It's only important that God knows who they are, and why they have been marked.

Sealed means secured, preserved, or protected, **not** necessarily *"saved"* at this time. We **can't** make that assumption yet. The salvation of the 144,000 will be confirmed at a later point in time.

This seal on the 144,000 means that they have been set apart, and protected from any harm that could be coming their way; but why are the 144,000 so special?

The 144,000 are "true Jews" having no Gentile blood mixed into them through intermarriage. In the end times they will legally represent, and identify the true nation of Israel. When they accept Jesus they will qualify to be the **first fruits** unto God and the Lamb. *Rev.14:4*

Next is the second of three multitudes in John's vision that suddenly shows up in heaven.

Rev.7: 9-10 *After this, John suddenly sees a multitude, which no man could number, standing before the throne from every nation, kindred, people, and tongue clothed in white.* Anytime a new group shows up in heaven we need to know who they are because if they are raptured saints, that would change the whole time line of this study.

Rev.7: 13-17 one of the elders asks John, *"What are all these people doing here, and where did they come from?"* John says, "Sir, you know", and the elder said, *"These are they which **came out of great tribulation**, and have washed their robes, and made them white in the blood of the Lamb. They will never hunger, or thirst again, and God will wipe away all their tears."*

Note: If these believers have come out of great tribulation, guess what? **They must have been in it** during the opening of the first six seals in Ch.6.

We **cannot** assume that these tribulation martyrs are in heaven because they were raptured. Most likely they were martyred for refusing the mark of the beast. Many of them died from hunger and thirst because they could not buy or sell without the mark of the beast. Remember: the rider on the "pale horse" was given power to kill ¼ of the world's population. *Rev.6:8*

They will be martyred in large numbers (millions worldwide) during the first 3 ½ years of the tribulation while the antichrist is actively pursuing his One World agenda. These would include the souls of the martyrs who were under the altar which is before the throne of God. They were slain for the word of God, and for their testimony. They were pleading for justice at the feet of God. *Rev.6: 9-11*

If this huge group of believers were raptured before the 7 years of tribulation began, then they could **not** have come out of the great tribulation as the elder said they did.

Some might wonder if this huge group of believers who were martyred might have been saved after the pre-tribulation rapture took place. My question to them would be: Who will lead them to the Lord if all Gentile believers are gone from the earth? Their answer would probably be: the two witnesses in Ch.11.

After all these centuries, isn't it more likely that God would be willing to postpone the rapture 3 ½ more years to include all of those new believers that will be saved as a result of hearing the two witnesses preach during the first 3 ½ years of tribulation? *Rev.11:3*

If they were frightened into seeking Jesus because all believers are suddenly gone, then how will the faith of these baby Christians be so well developed in that short 3 ½ year period of time, and in such an hostile environment, that they will become the source of all the millions of martyrs mentioned in Revelation.

Was it too late for people to come into Noah's ark after God closed the door? Yes! Once God closes the door it's no longer time for more people to be saved; it's time for His judgment to begin, and that judgment will be the undiluted wrath of God. If people are saved after the rapture, and during His wrath, then the wrath of God would be diluted.

This is the second of 3 huge groups that suddenly show up in heaven in John's vision. In this group are the millions who have died as a result of refusing to take the mark of the beast. The first group was primarily Old Testament believers who were already in heaven when John was called up, and given the vision.

This completes chapter 7. Chapter 8 begins the second 3 ½ years with the opening of the seventh, and last seal.

However, since our study is designed to divide the seven years of tribulation into two parts, so that we can study each half by itself, we will put chapters 8 and 9 on hold, because they are part of the second half (The wrath of God). We will jump to Ch.10 because it is part of the first 3 ½ years of the tribulations.

REVELATION Chapter 10
The Edible Book

Rev.10: 1 *John sees a mighty angel descend from heaven. His appearance was very bright, and he was arrayed in splendor.* This is a glorious and powerful angel.

Rev.10: 2 *He held in his hand a little scroll (opened). His right foot was set on the sea, and his left foot on land.* What is the implication?

One foot on the sea, and the other on land could imply that this mighty angel is staking a claim to the earth, since the entire surface of the world is basically comprised of water and land.

Rev.10: 3 *he roared like a lion standing over its' prey*, daring anyone to challenge his claim.

Rev.10: 8 the voice from heaven tells John to *"Go take the little scroll, which is open, out of the hand of the mighty angel that stands on the sea and the earth."*

Rev.10: 9-10 When John asks for the scroll, the angel tells him to *"take it and eat it up; and it will make your belly bitter, but it will be sweet as honey in your mouth."*

John took the scroll and ate it up. It was sweet in his mouth, but made his belly bitter. The question is: What is this little scroll, and what information does it contain? The best way to answer this is to use related scripture.

Ezekiel 2: 8-10 / 3: 1-3 says this *"Son of man, hear what I say unto you; do not rebel like that rebellious house: (Israel) open your mouth, and eat what I give you. And when I looked, behold, a hand stretched out to me; and in it a scroll, and he spread it before me (He opened it); and it was* *written on both sides: and there was written words of lamentations, and mourning, and woe."*

The little scroll, most likely is the "Word of God". Though it contains the sweetness of the wisdom and true promises of God, it also contains lamentations, judgments, warnings, and woes about the wrath of God upon the wicked kingdoms of this world.

For example: *Psalms 119:103* speaks of the sweetness of God's word: *How sweet are thy words unto my taste! Yea, sweeter than honey in my mouth!* And in contrast; the entire books of *Jeremiah and Lamentation*.

Rev.10: 11 John is told that *he must prophecy to many people, nations, tongues, and kings.* The question is: How can John be expected to do this; he is elderly, and he is exiled to the small island of Patmos in the Aegean Sea?

Bibles will still be available in the end times. The remainder of John's writings will contain prophecies to peoples, nations, tongues, and kings. His writings are now seen in five books of our present Bible. John wrote I, II, III John, the Gospel of John, and Revelation. How these books got off the island of Patmos is a mystery, but obviously they did, and thankfully we are blessed by them today. It's likely that the apostle John may have been released from his exile before he died; based on *III John Verses 13-14*.

III John Verses 13-14 *I had many things to write, but I will not with ink and pen write unto you: But I trust I shall shortly see you, and we shall speak face to face. Peace be to you. Our friends salute you. Greet the friends by name.*

REVELATION Chapter 11
The TWO WITNESSES

First 3 ½ years of the tribulation

Rev.11: 1 *In John's vision he is told to measure the temple of God, the altar, and those who worship there.* The question is: How do you measure people who worship?

Usually, when measurements are taken in the Bible, it is to annualize, and evaluate the spiritual condition of the people of God. For example: The plumb line in the book of *Amos Ch.* 7: 8 represented the accuracy of God's word; the standard of truth by which Israel could **gauge** themselves spiritually. Another example is Rom.3:23; *all have sinned and come* **short** *of the glory of God.* Rom.12: 3 *God has dealt to every man a* **measure** *of faith.* In this case the spiritual condition of God's people is "spiritually asleep."

This temple that John is told to measure is **not** yet built in Jerusalem, but John is seeing it in the future, and he is told to measure and evaluate it.

Rev.11: 2 *John is told* **not** *to measure outside of the temple, because it is given to the Gentiles, and they shall tread the holy city under foot for 3 ½ years.*

The question is: What is keeping these Gentiles in, and around the Holy City (Jerusalem) for 3 ½ years? Why are they there?

They are there to protect the Jews in Jerusalem so they can safely build their temple. Both the Jews and the antichrist want this temple built, but for two completely different reasons. The Jews want it built so they can resume worship and sacrifices as they are steeped in the Mosaic Laws. The antichrist wants the temple built in Jerusalem so he can eventually take it over by force.

After the antichrist fosters a 7 year peace treaty with the Jews, the armed forces of the antichrist surround the city to protect the Jews from belligerent Arabs. The Jews will begin to build their temple in Jerusalem; a temple that the antichrist secretly intends to hijack for his own use as soon as it is finished.

Israel will be completely unaware of this because they will think the antichrist is their Messiah (Savior) they have been waiting for ever since they rejected Jesus.

Rev.11: 3-4 speak of *two consecrated witnesses sent by God who are clothed in sackcloth*, implying that they, like John the Baptist; have no interest in material gain. Their motives are pure as they oppose the antichrist, and preach the gospel around the world by Satellite television *Matt.24:14*.

When these two witnesses preach the gospel, the whole world will listen because of their boldness in opposing the antichrist. They are the only ones who can get away with it. It's true that the Christian community should preach the gospel around the world, and we do make a valiant effort, but how much of the world is actually listening and responding? This is not saying anything against the awesome work that missionaries do, but they will never have a bully pulpit to oppose the antichrist like these two witnesses will have. Nor will they have a pulpit of power to preach the gospel around the world with all the media coverage that will be given to these two witnesses. So these are two very important men.

Some speculate that these two witnesses will be Elijah and Enoch; the only two people recorded in the Bible who have never died. Both were simply *"caught up" to heaven, although, "it's appointed to everyone once to die" Heb. 9:27*. They will eventually die at the hands of the antichrist. *Rev.11:7*.

Some speculate the two anointed ones will be Elijah and Moses because of the similar types of miracles that Moses did in Egypt.

Rev.11: 5-6 says: *And if any man shall hurt them, fire proceeds out of their mouth, and devours their enemies: and if any man shall hurt them, he must in this manner be killed. These have power to shut heaven that it rain not in the days of their prophecy: and have power over waters to turn them to blood, and to smite the earth with all plagues, as often as they will.*

These two witnesses have power to shut the heavens that it rain not in the days of their prophecy. What are the days of their prophecy? A. The first 3 ½ years.

It's likely that there will be a worldwide drought the first 3 ½ years of the tribulation, and that might be one more reason for wars, rumors of wars, and rationings of water, and other goods.

The two witnesses will stand up for God, and against the antichrist for the first 3 ½ years. It's an ironic situation because of the seven year treaty. While the temple is being built, the Jews are being protected by the same people who will later try to destroy them.

Most of the people around the world will be constantly watching by Satellite TV. They will be torn as to where to place their loyalty. Should they side with these two powerful men of God who do miracles, and preach their hearts out to a world where the love of many has grown cold, **or**....

Should they side with this charismatic world statesman who seems to have a lot of new ideas for how to solve the world's problems? However, he tends to speak outrageous things against God, and insists on everyone taking an identifying mark.

The two witnesses will stand up for God, and against the antichrist for the first 3 ½ years, while their temple is being built in the background. The antichrist wants to kill these two witnesses to shut them up, but he can't do it yet for three reasons. They are too popular, too powerful, and he has made a peace treaty with Israel for 7 years.

Rev.11: 7 *When they finish their testimony after 3 ½ years, the antichrist will make war with them and kill them,* as his forces hijack the newly finished temple.

Rev.11: 8-10 to the world it seems the antichrist has prevailed over these two men of God who have been tormenting, and convicting their conscience. Because now there seems to be a clear winner, millions more will take the mark of the beast.

Although millions have been saved by their powerful preaching, *most of the world is happy about the deaths of the two witnesses, and will* **not** *even allow their bodies to be buried. In fact the world celebrates as their* *dead bodies lie in the streets of Jerusalem for 3 ½ days;* and in the hot sun we might add.

While their dead bodies lie in the streets of Jerusalem, the antichrist's forces will hijack the temple, stop the Jewish sacrifices, and set up the abominable image of the beast; which is likely to be a man made idol that the world will be commanded to worship.

Rev.12: 7- 8 (Paraphrased) this is probably when *war breaks out in heaven between Michael and his angels; and the dragon and his angels, and the dragon prevails **not**; neither was there place found any more in heaven. And the great dragon was cast out to the earth, and his angels with him.*

Rev.12: 12-13 (paraphrased) *when the dragon saw that he was cast into the earth, he was very angry, and he persecuted the woman (Israel) which brought forth the man child (Jesus).*

Daniel 11: 31-37 gives us a blow by blow description of the hijacking of the temple.

Dan.11: 31 *His armed forces will raise up to desecrate the temple fortress, and will abolish the daily sacrifice. Then they will set up the abomination that causes desolation;* which most likely is the image of the beast. *(An idol)*

Dan.11: 33 Jewish elders will vehemently object, and try to regain control, but they will be killed or incarcerated.

The image of the beast could be quickly relocated to the newly built temple from another location; perhaps a country from within the former Roman Empire because that's where the antichrists headquarter city is likely to be located. The antichrist will then proclaim himself as God.

Dan.11: 36-37 *the antichrist will do according to his own will; he shall exalt and magnify himself above every god, and shall speak outrageous things against the God of gods.* He will think he is top dog; and that he has just conquered the world.

2 Thess. 2: 4 speaking of the antichrist says: *He will oppose, and will exalt himself over everything that is called God, or is worshipped; so that he sets himself up in God's temple, proclaiming himself to be God.*

At this time the 144,000 Jews are stunned because they now know that they have been deceived by the antichrist; and that the two witnesses were right about Jesus being their Messiah. They will also realize that the antichrist's forces have them surrounded in a killing field. What can they do? How can they escape?

Rev.11: 11 *after 3 ½ days the spirit of life from God enters into the two witnesses, and they stand up. Great fear falls on all those who see them.*

Great fear indeed! These men had power over all plagues. Millions more took the mark of the beast, and celebrated while their dead bodies lie in the streets of Jerusalem for 3 ½ days, and now they are standing up for all the world to see on Satellite TV.

They showed contempt for these two witnesses by **not** allowing their dead bodies the dignity of a descent burial. They've got to be horrified as to what will happen to them now that these two are alive and standing up?

Rev.11: 12 *the two witnesses heard a great voice from heaven say unto* **them** *"COME UP HERE" and* **they** *ascended to heaven in a cloud as their enemies watched.* The term *"COME UP HERE"* is **not** in reference to the rapture of all believers. The great voice is only calling the two witnesses to come up.

Rev.11: 13 *immediately after the "catching away" of the two witnesses, there is a great earthquake in Jerusalem that destroys 1/10 of the city and kills 7000 people.* Many of the 7000 will be Gentiles who were there treading down the holy city for 3 ½ years. *V.2*

The Gentiles were surrounding Jerusalem to enforce a 7 year peace treaty. They were there to protect Jews from belligerent Arabs while the Jews build their temple during the first 3 ½ years of the tribulation. *Luke 21:20*

The powerful testimonies of the two witnesses for 3 ½ years, followed by *this devastating earthquake, frightens the* **remnant** *so much that they begin to glorify the God of heaven.*

Who is the remnant?

Rom.9: 27 *Isaiah also cried concerning Israel, though the number of the children of Israel be as the sand of the sea, a* **remnant** *shall be saved.*

The remnant is the 144,000 true Jews who were sealed, and protected, but not necessarily saved in chapter 7. At that time they were sealed from harm, but not unto salvation.

But now…. Praise God, here in Ch.11, this is the point at which the elect of Israel are finally saved after all these centuries of rejecting Jesus as their Messiah. This is an amazing time in the history of the world!

"*Rev.11: 13*" is the first record of the 144,000 giving glory to the God of heaven. Up to this point they were steeped in the Old Testament law, and willing to accept the antichrist as their Messiah. In this future scenario, the Jewish people are finally awakening from their spiritual slumber.

They are finally rejecting the antichrist as their Messiah, because he has set up a despicable idol in their temple, and accepting Jesus Christ, because of the powerful testimony of the two witnesses, and the ensuing earthquake.

Isaiah 66: 8 *Who hath heard such a thing? Who hath seen such things? Shall the earth be made to bring forth in one day? Or shall a nation be born at once; for as soon as Zion travailed, she brought forth her children.*

God sealed the 144,000 in their foreheads with His own name "*Yahweh*"*,* probably just before the 7 year treaty was signed with the antichrist, and that is why the 144,000 Jews will **not** have the mark of the beast. The 144,000 are "true Jews" having no Gentile blood mixed into them, and therefore **as believers**, they now qualify to be the **first fruits** unto God, and the Lamb.

Rom.1: 16 says *the **gospel of Christ** is the power of God, unto salvation, to everyone that believes,* **to the Jew first,** (first fruits) *and also to the Greek.* (Gentiles)

The 144,000 are the first fruit unto God, but the worldwide church (body of believers) is the main harvest. It is comprised mostly of Gentiles. The 144,000 Jews must be approved by God first before the Gentiles can be raptured when the earth is harvested.

Now that the 144,000 true Jews are saved, and will **not** lose their salvation, the rest is academic. Satan can no longer save himself from the lake of fire by deceiving the Jews as to whom their Messiah is. Now Satan's only hope of **foiling** God's most important unfulfilled prophecy is to destroy them. God's most important unfulfilled prophecy is:

Ezekiel 37: 27-28 it says this: *My tabernacle also shall be with them: yea, I will be their God, and they shall be my people. And the heathen shall know* *that I the Lord do sanctify Israel, when my sanctuary shall be in the midst of them for evermore.*

In this future scenario the 144,000 true Jews will recognize Jesus as their Messiah. Israel recognizing Jesus as their Messiah is the main reason for the 7 years of tribulation which is designed to awaken them from their spiritual slumber *Romans 11: 7-8.*

John 1: 10-11 When Jesus came the first time, *He came to His own, and His own people recognized Him **not*** (as their Messiah), but now they do. Now it's a whole new ball game between God and Satan.

When Satan can no longer deceive the Jews, then his only other option will be to destroy them so that Jesus **cannot** reign over them on this earth when He returns. This is in reference to the millennial reign of Christ.

Next we must study Matthew Chapter 24, the "Mt. Olivet" discourse, because now that the 144,000 Jews are saved, and have seen the abomination of desolation sitting in the newly built temple in Jerusalem, they must flee from the killing field they are in. The before mentioned earthquake will make their escape possible.

It's likely that this earthquake will hit the edge of town, and take out one section (1/10th) of that circumference. This could have a devastating effect on the antichrist forces that are surrounding the holy city. This earthquake could provide the Jews an escape route from this killing field they are in, if they move quickly *Rev.11:13.*

While the Gentiles forces of the antichrist will be in total disarray during the earthquake, many of the Jews will know exactly what they must do, because the two witnesses will have already warned them to flee at that time.

Matt.24: 15-18 says: *When ye therefore shall see the abomination of desolation, spoken of by Daniel the prophet, stand in the holy place, then let them which be in Judea flee into the mountains: Let him which is on the housetop not come down to take anything out of his house: Neither let him which is in the field return back to take his clothes.*

Now our study must move to the gospel of Matthew chapter 24 to see a more detailed account of *"The Great Escape"* of the 144,000 true Jews from the killing field they are in; when the antichrist hi-jacks their newly built temple, and tries to destroy them.

MATTHEW Chapter 24

The Mt. Olivet Discourse

Beginning of Sorrows

First 3 ½ years of the tribulation

Matt.24: 1-3 His disciples asked Him *"what is the sign of your coming, and of the end of the world?"* When the Scribes and Pharisees asked for a sign Jesus said, *there shall no sign be given, but the sign of the prophet Jonas;* (which was preaching).

But His disciples wanted a sign so they could be prepared in a time of persecution, and not deceived, so Jesus gives them a full explanation.

Matt.24: 4-6 Jesus answer to His disciples is: *let no one deceive you for many shall come in my name, saying, I am Christ, and shall deceive many.* Hopefully, not true Christians. *You shall hear of wars and rumors of wars, be not troubled, the end is not yet.*

Matt.24: 7-8 *There will be famines, and pestilence,* (often the results of war), *but there will also be natural phenomenon such as volcanoes, and earthquakes. These are only the beginning of sorrows.*

So there will be a time of trouble before the 7 years of tribulation begins. It will be like a giant spring being wound tighter and tighter, more and more tension each day. Then when the spring is sprung, the tribulation will begin.

Matt.24: 9 *Then shall they deliver you up,* ("You" the underground church hiding to avoid having to take the mark of the beast) *to be afflicted, and killed, and you shall be hated of all nations for my names' sake.* There is a time coming when Christianity will be vilified around the world. Because true Christians will not cooperate, or take the mark of the beast, they will be labeled "enemies of the state", or even "enemies of humanity".

Matt.24: 10 *Then comes the falling away of the churches in general around the world. Gripped with fear, to protect themselves, they will turn one another over to the authorities.* In every church there are strong Christians and weak Christians. The weak and fearful will turn in the strong and faithful. The weak and fearful will be the first to cave in. Using membership rolls: entire congregations could be captured, or killed.

Matt.10: 18-20 says *"you shall be brought before governors and kings for my sake, for a testimony against them and the Gentiles. But when they deliver you up, take no thought how or what you shall speak: for it shall be given you in that same hour what you shall speak. It is not you that speak, but the Spirit of your Father that speaks in you.*

Matt.24: 11 *and many false prophets shall arise* (including the antichrist's right hand man), *and shall deceive many* with **lying words and wonders**. The antichrist and the false prophet are illusionists trying to pass off illusions as legitimate miracles.

Matt.24: 12-13 Sin, crime, and corruption will be so prevalent at that time that it will be difficult to trust anyone. Compassion will be rare. *The love of many will grow cold. V.14 and this gospel of the kingdom shall be preached in all the world* (even during this time of tribulation) *for a witness to all nations; and then shall the end come.*

We normally think of the modern day Christian church as being commissioned to preach the gospel around the world, but this is more likely to be in reference to the two witnesses that God will send. ***They*** will preach the gospel around the world at that time.

The two witnesses of God will preach the gospel for the first 3 1/2 years on the streets of Jerusalem as they oppose the antichrist. That will take a lot of chutzpah. The whole world will be watching by Satellite TV, because they are bold enough to stand against the antichrist.

Why can't the antichrist stop them; because the antichrist has fostered a peace treaty with the Jews for 7 years? No one has ever been able to do this before. This allows the Jews time to build their temple, and begin sacrificing. The Jews will think of the antichrist as their long awaited Messiah, and protector.

But after 3 1/2 years when the temple is finished, he will kill the two witnesses, break the treaty, and takes charge of the temple by force to exalt himself as God *II Thess. 2: 4.*

Matt.24: 15-16 (At mid-tribulation) *when you see the abomination of desolation spoken of in Daniel, stand in the holy place, then let them which are in Judea flee to the mountains;* possibly to a vast network of deep underground nuclear bomb shelters. These shelters are already built, and well supplied with food and air, beneath the mountains of Israel.

Jews who are no longer deceived as to whom their Messiah is, and now *saved by the grace of God*, must flee to the mountains without delay, or be killed by the forces of the antichrist who are surrounding the city of Jerusalem *Rev.11: 2*.

But how will they flee if they are surrounded by the forces of the antichrist in a killing field? The answer is in **Rev.11: 13**. *Immediately after the "catching away" of the two witnesses, there is a great earthquake in Jerusalem that destroys 1/10 of the city and kills 7000 people.* Many of the 7000 will be Gentiles who were there treading down the Holy City for 3 ½ years *Rev.11:2*.

The Gentiles were surrounding Jerusalem to enforce a 7 year peace treaty. They are there to protect Israel from belligerent Arabs while the Jews build their temple.

It's likely that this earthquake will hit the edge of town, and take out one section, 1/10 of that circumference. This earthquake could provide the Jews an escape route from this killing field they are in, if they move quickly.

While the Gentiles forces of the antichrist will be in total disarray, many of the Jews will know exactly what to do, because the two witnesses will have already warned them.

It could be that people will be on their housetops watching the temple being built, or in their fields working when they are informed on their cell phones of the takeover of the temple by the antichrist. They will need to immediately take the appropriate action. ***They must flee*** to the mountain bomb shelters.

Matt.24: 15-18 says: *When you shall see the abomination of desolation, spoken of by Daniel the prophet, stand in the holy place, then let them which* *be in Judea flee into the mountains: Let him which is on the housetop* **not** *come down to take anything out of his house: Neither let him which is in the field return back to take his clothes.*

Luke 17: 34-36 *I tell you, in that night there shall be two men in one bed; the one shall be taken, and the other one left. Two women shall be grinding together; the one shall be taken, and the other left. Two men shall be in the field; the one shall be taken, and the other left.* Q. Is this the rapture? A. No.

These verses are **not** referring to the rapture of the saints, but rather to the Jewish people in Jerusalem who must flee to the mountains mentioned in Matt.24:15-16 for protection from the forces of the antichrist. The antichrist has, no doubt, ordered anyone without the mark to be arrested.

Jewish people who **did** take the mark of the beast will be *"left"* alone because they believed the antichrist was their Messiah, and willingly received the mark. Antichrist is **not** going to arrest his committed friends.

Jewish people who **did not** take the mark will be *"taken"* at that time regardless of the 7 year treaty that was designed to protect them. When the antichrist breaks that treaty he will try to capture as many of them as he can before they escape to the wilderness. Here is his big chance to wipe out the 144,000 Jews who represent the nation of Israel.

Despite their former loyalty to the antichrist, the 144,000 Jews will **not** have the mark of the beast because they were already marked in their foreheads with the seal of God in Ch.7: 2-4.

Luke 17: 37 Jesus disciples ask him, *"Where Lord"* will they be taken? Jesus answers, *"Wherever the body is, there will the eagles* (Scavengers in this case) *be gathered together.* Most likely their bodies will be taken to a garbage dump, and left for the vultures and scavengers.

The 144,000 Jews and those who escaped will be protected in the mountains for the **last** 3.5 years of the great tribulation according to Rev.12:6. Note that if even one of those 144,000 is captured, and killed by the antichrist, it's "game over, Satan wins." Legally there must be exactly 12,000 from each tribe.

We can account for the 144,000 Jews in the first 3 ½ years of the tribulation while the temple is being built, **and** the second 3 ½ years when they are protected in a wilderness hideout. Even though the 144,000 have accepted Christ they will remain on earth the entire seven years of the tribulation.

After the 144,000 Jews have accepted Jesus as their Messiah, the rapture can occur to take mainly Gentile believers out of harms way, just prior to the wrath of God on the unbelievers who are left behind.

Matt.24: 21 *Then shall be great tribulation such as was not since the beginning of the world to this time.* God's wrath comes in the second 3 1/2 years of tribulation.

The 144,000 may have missed the rapture by God's design for two reasons. First, because Gentile believers are God's **spiritually** chosen people, while Jews are God's **earthly** chosen people. The second reason is best explained in Matt.24:22.

Matt.24: 22 *except those days be shortened, no flesh would be saved, but for the elect's sake, they will be shortened* (To 3 ½ years). The elect are the 144,000 Jewish believers who will still be on earth, protected by God, during the last 3 1/2 years of the tribulation. If it weren't for God protecting them, all flesh would be destroyed.

If God in His wrath destroyed all flesh at that time, there would be no tribulation survivors to inhabit the earth during the millennial reign of Christ.

Matt. 24: 23-26 Jesus is warning these protected Jews *"If anyone shall say to you, Lo, here is Christ or there; check out his signs and wonders.* **Do not believe them.***"*

Why not? It is a trick designed to draw the Jews out of hiding where they are being fed, and protected; most likely in nuclear bomb shelters under the mountains of Israel for the last 3.5 years of the great tribulation *Rev.12:14;* **they must stay put.**

REVELATION Chapter 12

THE WOMAN (Israel)

Neither the wrath of God nor the rapture has occurred yet in this study.

Rev.12: 1 *There appeared a great wonder in heaven; a* **woman** *clothed with the sun, and the moon under her feet, and on her head a crown of 12 stars.* Who is this woman? The way to uncover this symbolism is to use related scripture. Joseph had a dream in Gen. 37.

Gen.37: 9-10 (paraphrased). *He (*Joseph*) dreamed another dream, and told it to his eleven brothers, and said "The Sun, and the moon, and the eleven stars* **bowed down** *to me." And he told it to his father and his father* **rebuked** *him and said "Shall I and your mother and your brethren indeed bow down unto you?*

The question is: In Joseph's dream, who does the sun, moon, and 11 stars represent?

They represent Joseph's father, mother, and 11 brothers, the sons of Jacob. So, Jacob himself interprets who the sun, moon, and stars are. But who is the woman?

Q. What nation emerged from this family? Gen.35:10-12 tells us that God changed Jacob's name to **Israel.** Can we conclude that **the woman** in verse 1 with the sun, moon, and 12 stars might **symbolize the nation of Israel?**

Rev.12: 2-5 *She* (Israel) *being with child cried, travailing in birth, and pain to be delivered. She gave birth to a* **son** *who was to rule all nations with a rod of iron.* Here again we need to use related scripture.

Psalms 2: 7-9 (Paraphrased) the Lord has promised; you are my Son. I will give you the nations, and you will rule them with a rod of iron. So, can we conclude that **the son** born of the woman (Israel) in verse 2 **symbolizes Jesus?**

Rev.12: 3 *there appears another wonder in heaven; behold a great red dragon having 7 heads, 10 horns, and 7 crowns.*

Rev.12: 9 says, *the great dragon was cast out, that old serpent called the Devil and Satan.* Can we conclude that the **great red dragon** in verse 3 is **symbolic of Satan?**

Rev.12: 3 says "The dragon has 7 heads, 10 horns, and 7 crowns." Let's put this on hold to avoid teaching it repetitiously, because we will get into this same symbolism when we get to *Chapter 13 and 17*.

Rev.12: 4a In John's vision of the future he sees *the Dragon's tail drew 1/3 of the stars of heaven and cast them to the earth.* **Rev.1: 20** we learned that stars can mean angels.

The dragon's tail **drew** 1/3 of the angels of heaven, and cast them to the earth. But please don't think of his tail like a broom that swept 1/3 of the angels out of heaven at random.

The original meaning of the word **drew** is not to sweep like a broom, but to hale, call, draw, or draft, and when Satan "haled them" his angels followed him to the earth. They had a choice to follow or not. This probably happened at the beginning of the creation.

Rev.12: 4b In this Ch.12 scenario a major event is about to happen on earth, and Satan wants all his forces on hand to help him destroy this man-child that's about to be delivered by the woman (Israel). This might be in reference to the birth of Jesus.

Rev.12: 5 *She (Israel) delivers a son who will rule all nations with a rod of iron, but her son was caught up unto the throne of God.*

Satan failed to destroy Jesus at birth when King Herod ordered all baby boys in the area of Bethlehem less than 2 years of age to be killed. *However*, Jesus did give up His life on the cross, and then He was resurrected (caught up) to the right hand throne of God.

Rev.12: 6-9 *War breaks out in heaven between the dragon, plus one third of the angels, and Michael, plus the remaining two thirds of the angels, and Michael (The archangel) wins.* Satan will be demoted, and apparently Michael will be promoted to his place as the chief ranking angel. From that time on Satan (the accuser of the brethren) will have **no more** access to heaven.

Until that point in time Satan will continue to have full access to come and go between earth and heaven, and to make accusations against believers before the throne of God. That's what Satan does now, night and day. V.10

Rev.12: 10 Satan is allowed to keep his place in heaven even after his fall, just as man kept earth after his fall. But at this time **in the future**, he and his angels will be permanently banned from heaven. Cast down to the earth, never to return to heaven.

The reason Satan is still allowed access to heaven is because God has not yet fulfilled all of His prophetic promises to the Jewish people. Therefore, God has not yet proven that He is not a liar on the same level as the devil.

Rev.12: 11-12 *you who dwell in heaven, rejoice! Because Satan* (the accuser), *and his angels are permanently gone. The Devil is come down to earth with great wrath because he knows his time is short.*

His time is short to do what? To destroy God's people, the Jews, before he's bound, and cast into the bottomless pit for 1000 years *Rev.20:1-3*. Satan knows scripture, so he knows this is going to happen to him. His time is short to destroy the Jewish people.

All prophecy in scripture pertains to the Jewish people. **If** Satan can foil God's prophecies, and promises to the Jewish people then, God would become a liar like Satan is.

If that could be true, God would **not** be able to legally condemn Satan to the lake of fire where he will be tormented day and night forever and ever *Rev.20:10*. The Lake of Fire is Satan's greatest fear!

Rev.12: 13-14 *tell us the dragon is very angry about being cast out of heaven to earth, and begins to persecute the woman (Israel). But the woman is given two wings of a great eagle to fly into the wilderness where she is nourished, and protected for the last 3 ½ years of the tribulation.* Their hide out could be the nuclear bomb shelters under the mountains of Israel where they could have plenty of food and air for 3 ½ years.

This is the great escape that Israel made from the killing field in Chapter 11. It was facilitated by an earthquake.

Eagle's wings in scripture are usually symbolic of ***divine deliverance.*** Two eagle wings are given to the woman (Israel). *Isaiah 40:31 also Exodus 19:4*

Exodus 19: 4 says *you have seen what I did unto the Egyptians, and how I bare you on eagles' wings, and brought you unto myself.*

Notice that in verses 13 and 14 the woman (Israel) is protected in a wilderness hideout for the last 3 ½ years of the tribulation, implying that Israel is still here on earth for the entire 7 years of the tribulation *Rev.12: 6*, the 144,000 are among this group.

REVELATION Chapter 13 A
Antichrist (beast) Revealed

First 3 ½ of the tribulation

Neither the rapture, nor the wrath of God has yet occurred in this study. We must go back to the beginning of the 7 years of the tribulation in order to study the emergence of the antichrist.

Rev. 13: 1 *In John's vision he sees a beast rise up out of the sea having* **seven heads, ten horns, and ten crowns.** This is not likely to be a sea of water that would produce such a beast.

Rev. 17: 15 tells John *"**the waters** you saw **are people, multitudes, nations, and languages**".* Therefore, it's more likely that the beast came up out of the sea of humanity.

The beast is human, but symbolically he has 7 heads, 10 horns, and ten crowns. The word "beast", does not refer to his appearance, but to his character. He is a monster in disguise.

Let's deal first with the 10 horns, and the 10 crowns, and then we'll deal with the 7 heads.

Dan. 7: 24a informs us that *the 10 horns are 10 kings.* They represent a coalition of 10 end-time kingdoms. Each kingdom will be composed of many countries. They are 10 kings with 10 crowns that are led by, and coordinated by the antichrist. As we continue to study Revelation we will hear more and more about these 10 world kingdoms.

Dan. 7: 24b informs us that this coalition will begin with 10 distinct world kingdoms, but will be temporarily reduced to 7 when the "little horn" (antichrist) uproots 3 of them.

Most likely the three kings that were uprooted were **not** in full compliance with the antichrist's "One World" agenda. Rev.17:12-14 implies that the three uprooted kings will be replaced before the attack on Israel begins at Armageddon. Therefore, I may refer to them in the future as 10 world kingdoms instead of 7.

Rev.17: 12-13 says: *And the* **ten horns** *which you saw* **are ten kings**, *which have received no kingdom as yet; but receive power as kings one hour with the beast. These have one mind, and shall give their power and strength unto the beast.*

In a very brief meeting with the antichrist, these ten evil men will be appointed kings over the 10 kingdom coalition, and will swear total allegiance to him.

The 10 horns and 10 crowns are 10 world kingdoms; each composed of many countries. Now let's deal with the 7 heads of the beast that came up from the sea of humanity.

Rev.17: 9 states that *the 7 heads are 7 hills on which the woman sits*. The woman in Ch.12 was symbolic of Israel, but this woman is symbolic of evil.

We will learn later in Ch.17 that **this woman is symbolic of an evil world system.**

She is Mystery Babylon, the great harlot; possibly the headquarter city of the antichrist.

Mystery Babylon will probably be located somewhere in the former Roman Empire, and will be supported by these 10 world kingdoms. They will all send financial support to this city, and she will become very rich. **Rome Italy is known as, "the city on seven hills."**

We will learn more about the 7 hills on which the harlot sits in Ch.17, but for now let's study the: **Characteristics of the antichrist.**

Dan.7: 8 He begins as *a little horn* (king) *who has a mouth speaking great things.* (As in, outrageous things) He will be a dynamic, charismatic orator.

Dan.7: 25 For the entire first 3 ½ years of the tribulation *the antichrist will speak great words against the most high, and shall wear out the saints.*

It's much easier for him to make accusations against God, than it is for believers to defend against them.

He will threaten to change times and laws. This may also be wearisome to the saints because these will probably be "tried and true" traditions that need nothing changed; traditional Christian or Jewish holidays for example.

Dan.11: 36 states that this reprobate *will do according to his own will; he will arrogantly exalt and magnify himself, above every god, and speak against the God of gods.*

Dan.11: 37 tells us he will **not** regard the **"God of his fathers."** The word "God" is capitalized (KJV) implying that his fathers worshiped the right God. This could imply that he is Jewish. Jews are well known for keeping records of the God of their fathers.

It's not likely that Israel would ever consider anyone other than a Jew to be their Messiah. Old Testament prophecies spoke to the Jews about the coming of their Messiah through the blood line of King David, so they are expecting a Jewish Messiah.

Acts 3: 22 *For Moses truly said unto the fathers, A prophet shall the Lord your God raise up unto you of your brethren, like unto me; him shall you hear in all things whatsoever he shall say unto you.* So the Jews are **not** likely to accept a Gentile for their Messiah.

Daniel 11: 37 cont: *nor will he regard the desires of women.* This could imply that the antichrist is homosexual, or simply has very little respect for women.

Dan.9: 27 He will foster a peace treaty with Israel for one week of years (7 years), allowing them time to build their temple in Jerusalem. Then after 3 ½ years when the temple is finished, he will break the treaty, and take over the temple by force, to exalt himself as God. He is a liar and a truce breaker.

II Thess. 2: 4 speaking of the antichrist says: *Who opposes and exalts himself above all that is called God, or that is worshiped; so that he as God sits in the temple of God, showing himself that he is God.* He is an impostor. The term "anti" means against, but it also means "instead of."

Rev.11:7 He is the beast from the bottomless pit (From the pit of hell).

Rev. 13: 3 *one of the antichrist's heads will be **mortally** wounded, but the wound will be healed.* The world will think he is supernatural. It could be a failed assassination attempt by an overly zealous so called Christian, giving the antichrist a valid excuse to make war with the saints.

Possibly the head wound (assassination attempt) may have been to one of the antichrist's "doubles" (if he has them). Verse 3 says *"**one of his heads**" was wounded **to death**,* implying that he may use "look alike doubles."

Antichrist is a man. He does not have more than one head. Saddam Husain, former leader of Iraq, used several different lookalike doubles for public appearances due to assassination threats and attempts.

It's not likely that the antichrist was actually killed, and came back to life. It was an illusion. He does not have the power to lay down his life, and take it up again. Only Jesus can do that, because He is "the resurrection and the life" *John 11:25.*

But after the dead lookalike is discarded, the antichrist could have makeup artists take time laps photography of an artificial wound on his head that appears to progressively heal.

Rev. 13: 4 *the world begins to **worship** the dragon* (Satan) *that gave power to the beast, saying "Who is like the beast, and who is able to make war with him."* After all, he now appears to have power over life and death.

This tells us that the antichrist is likely to be a powerful global military leader, and has access to weapons of mass destruction. He is very intimidating, and there's no way to stop him.

Rev. 13: 5-6 *Satan gave the antichrist a mouth to speak blasphemies against God for 3 ½ years (Dan. 7:25).* How long was Jesus' earthly ministry? (3 1/2 years)

God is being very patient with the antichrist, because the 2 witnesses are preaching the gospel during the first 3 ½ years of the tribulation, and millions are being saved.

Rev. 13: 7 *Satan gives the antichrist power to make war with the saints, and to overcome them.* While the antichrist is verbally attacking God, and all who dwell in heaven, he is physically attacking the saints on earth.

For the antichrist to make war with the saints, they have to be present on this earth at the same time he is. The erroneous concept of a pre-tribulation rapture would make this impossible, because the saints would have already been removed. *Rev. 13: 7* also tells us *Satan gave the antichrist power over all kindred, tongues, and nations.* The entire world will be in his grip. His goal is to be the king of all the kings and kingdoms of the world. He would be a counterfeit king of kings and lord of lords.

Rev. 13: 8 *Most people who dwell on earth, whose names are **not** written in the Lamb's book of life, will worship the antichrist.* Those who oppose the antichrist are overcome, and martyred by the millions.

REVELATION Chapter 13 B
The False Prophet

The first 3 ½ years of the tribulation

Rev. 13: 11 *John sees another beast come up out of the earth.* The first beast came up from the sea of humanity. Why does this beast come up from the earth? I don't know for sure, but it implies that he is earthy or worldly.

I John 2:15 says: *Love not the world, neither the things that are in the world. If any man loves the world, the love of the Father is not in him.*

While the antichrist will be hung up on power over people, the false prophet might be obsessed with material things. That's why he's so good at illusions, and lying wonders.

He had two horns like a lamb implying that he is less threatening than the first beast which had 10 horns. This beast has only two, like a lamb, *and yet he speaks as a dragon.*

Rev. 13: 12 He is actually just as dangerous as the antichrist, because *he exercises all the power of the first beast, and causes all the earth to worship the beast.* How? He gives credibility to the antichrist. The first beast (antichrist) is a political leader; the second beast (the false prophet) is a religious leader. That's why he's called a prophet.

The antichrist might have Jewish ancestors because it's **not** likely that Israel would ever consider anyone other than a Jew to be their Messiah. If the antichrist is Jewish then it's likely that the false prophet might be also.

Moses had Aaron (a priest) to speak for him, Jesus had John the Baptist (a preacher) to prepare the way for him, and the antichrist will have a spokesman (a prophet) to prepare the way for him, and to exalt, promote, and magnify his **false** glory.

Rev.13: 13 *the false prophet performs signs and wonders such as calling fire down from heaven,* but don't forget what is said in…

II Thess.2: 9-10 *Even him, whose coming is after the working of Satan with all power and signs and lying wonders, and with all deceivableness and unrighteousness in them that perish;* **because they received not the love of the truth***, that they might be saved.*

By the power of Satan, the antichrist will perform signs and lying wonders. He and the false prophet are illusionists. They are masters of deception.

II Thess. 2: 11-12 *and for this cause,* "What cause?", *because they received not the love of the truth.* God first sent them truth by the two witnesses, but they hated the truth. So, *God shall send people strong delusions, that they should believe a lie: that they all might be damned who believed not the truth, but had pleasure in unrighteousness.*

Rev.13: 14 when most people of the earth are deceived, and awestruck by the so called "miracles", *the false prophet declares that they should* **make an image to the beast**, (it will also be an image *of* the beast) and he throws in this little caveat. *He reminds them of the mortal head wound received by the beast,* that was supernaturally healed. He seemed to have risen from the dead, a counterfeit to Christ's resurrection. So they make an image to the beast that could later become the abomination of desolation that is set up in the newly built temple, when the antichrist takes it over by force.

The antichrist hates Christians because it was probably an overly zealous "so called Christian" who tried to kill him with a sword to the head. It's a great excuse for him to vilify Christians; to target them, and make war with them *Rev.13: 7.*

Along with the 2 witnesses, Christians are his chief opposition until he finally just wears them out with relentless accusations against them, and the Most High God.

Rev.13: 15 *the false prophet had power to give life to the "image of the beast."* ***Stop, halt, time out, no way!*** As Christians we know that the false prophet **cannot** give life to anything, and certainly not to this inanimate, man-made object. Only God can give life. However, the false prophet could make it **appear** to have life. This is another one of his illusions.

The false prophet was given power to make the image of the beast speak. Since only people can speak, this implies that the image is in the form, and likeness of the antichrist. It is a very sophisticated computerized robot.

Making this robotic head speak **does not** just mean that the false prophet will put a speaker in the computer, but that he will program this computer to speak powerful charismatic words, and statements that will astonish people around the world.

Although they are partners, the false prophet might be the real brains behind the antichrist, and he plays him like a fiddle. The false prophet is a master manipulator.

No human being, other than Jesus Christ, could ever be smart enough to successfully be the king of the entire world; so the antichrist will utilize this powerful computer to assist him.

The latest state of the art technology will be used to make it so realistic that no one will be able to tell if it is the real antichrist, or his robotic image. Most of the world may **not** even believe that there is a robotic image of the antichrist, because it will be so realistic.

It will be equipped with a powerful computer that can make all of his sounds, expressions, and movements seem very realistic. Most of its technology will be behind walls or curtains.

With previously gathered data about those who accepted, or rejected the mark, this preprogrammed robotic "talking head" will have the ability to decide who lives, or dies based on their loyalty to the beast, and his One World agenda.

Jesus said *"He that is **not** with me is against me"* Matt.12:30. The antichrist will basically be saying the same thing by demanding that everyone take the mark of the beast; thereby identifying themselves with him by receiving the mark, **or** identifying themselves against him by refusing the mark.

Rev.13: 16-17 the ten king coalition, led by *the antichrist, causes all levels of society worldwide to take a mark in their right hand, or in their forehead. Without this mark they cannot buy or sell.....* That's a big problem. How will they obtain the necessities for life? How will they support their families?

The mark is likely to be an invisible type of bar code. Some type of a laser mark applied quickly, and painlessly, or possibly a computer chip applied hypodermically under the skin.

Many will take the mark voluntarily because it will be presented as a great idea for solving some of the world's most pressing problems, such as **catching criminals.** The first time they try to buy anything, the police will be there to arrest them.

Other uses might be to **find missing persons** such as children. Scanners will be installed in public places to help find kidnapped or run away children.

Authenticating people's identity: this worldwide system would be owned and operated by antichrist loyalists from one central location. It could be anywhere including Europe, or the United States.

Outside intervention into this secured system would be very difficult without giving up your own identification and location.

Buying and selling over the internet might require a web cam, or a web scan to complete the transaction. Lost or stolen credit cards could be a thing of the past in a cashless society. No one would need a credit card if they had an embedded chip.

Many will take the mark simply **out of fear** of not being able to buy or sell necessities such as groceries, medicine, utilities, fuel, and parts for vehicles, etc.

Unfortunately, some will accept the mark because their home church advised them it is okay. These will be churches that seldom study or teach the book of Revelation.

Some will refuse the mark of the beast because their home church will inform them of the dire warning expressed in Rev.14: 9-10

Rev.14: 9-10 If any man worship the beast and his image, and receive his mark in his forehead or in his hand, the same shall drink of the wine of the wrath of God, which is poured out without mixture into the cup of his indignation; and he shall be tormented with fire and brimstone in the presence of the holy angels, and in the presence of the Lamb.

These are powerful words: ***Under no circumstances should any believer willingly receive the mark of the beast.*** On judgment day we can trust that God will know who willingly took the mark of the beast, and who was tricked, coerced, or forced to take it.

The antichrist will require that everyone come on board. It will be mandated by law. Those who refuse will be hauled into court, warned, threatened, persecuted, and prosecuted. We can rest assured that the Lord will not leave us or forsake us at that time.

Matt.10: 18-20 says this *"You shall be brought before governors and kings for my sake, for a testimony against them and the Gentiles. But when they deliver you up, take no thought how or what you shall speak: for it shall be given you in that same hour what you shall speak. It is not you that speak, but the Spirit of your father which speaks in you."*

It's quite possible that believers who oppose the antichrist by refusing to take the "mark" during the tribulation will be threatened, arrested, tried, imprisoned, and at some point given **10 days to change their mind** before their head is removed.

Why 10 days? To answer this we must go to Rev.20:4 where it says; beheading is the method of execution that the antichrist will choose.

Rev.20: 4 John saw *the souls of them that were **beheaded** for the witness of Jesus and for the word of God, and which had **not** worshipped the beast or his image. They had **not** received his mark upon their foreheads or in their hand; they lived and reigned with Christ a thousand years.* This is a reference to the millennial reign of Christ, but why **10 days** to take the mark, or lose their head?

Rev.2: 10 says this: *"Fear none of those things which you shall suffer; behold the devil shall cast some of you into prison that you may be tried, and **you shall have tribulation 10 days: be faithful unto death, and I will give you a crown of life."***

At that time of mass martyrdom, **10 traumatic days** to decide to take the mark or lose their head, will be common knowledge to most people because they will have heard of it happening to so many other people.

John 16: 2 tells us there is a time coming that *whosoever kills a Jew or a Christian will think that he has done God a service.*

If these martyrs came out of the great tribulation, then guess what, they must have been in it. The rapture is not yet, neither is the wrath of God, but it's getting closer in this study.

The first 3 ½ years of the tribulation is **not** the wrath of God, but the wrath of the antichrist as he attempts to destroy anyone who stands in the way of his "One World Order." His goal is to be the king of all the kingdoms of the world. He would be a counterfeit king of kings.

Rev. 13: 18 the number of the beast, 666, is not sufficient to number all of earth's population, so it might be the antichrist's personal number. *It is the number of a man. (KJV)*

If the universal products code (UPC) is somehow used to mark all of earth's people, there would be plenty of numbers available to identify the entire population of the world.

Keep in mind that while the antichrist is putting more and more pressure on society, he is being opposed for 3 ½ years by the two witnesses. The world is in a quandary as to whom to give their loyalty; this antichrist (answer man), or these two powerful men of God.

The two witnesses were killed in Ch.11, but their ministry will be for the entire first 3 ½ years of the tribulation before they are killed. It's very likely that far more people will be lead to the Lord during these 3 ½ years of worldwide preaching, than any other 3 ½ year period in history.

The missionaries do a wonderful job, but they will never have a bully pulpit to oppose the antichrist like these two witnesses will have (with all the media coverage). Nor will they have such a pulpit of power as these two witnesses will have to preach the gospel around the world.

It is logical to think that the rapture of believers would take place after the first 3 ½ years of worldwide preaching, by these two witnesses, so that new converts could be included in the rapture. This would put the rapture near the middle of the 7 years of the tribulation.

REVELATION Chapter 14 A
The "Wave" Offering

Neither the rapture nor the wrath of God has yet occurred in this study.

Rev. 14: 1 John sees *a Lamb standing on Mt. Zion with 144,000 Jewish believers who have the Father's name etched in their foreheads.* This symbol may or may not be visible.

That's why the 144,000 who were once deceived by the antichrist will **not** have the mark of the beast. They already have "Yahweh" written on their forehead.

These are the same 144,000 who were sealed in their foreheads in chapter 7; a symbol of ownership. There were 12,000 from each of the 12 tribes of Israel *Rev. 7: 3, 4.*

The 144,000 are "True Jews" having no gentile blood mixed into them through inter-marriage. In the end times they will legally represent the nation of Israel; and therefore **as believers**, they will qualify to be the **first fruits** unto God and the Lamb.

Romans 1:16 tells us: *the power of God is unto salvation to everyone that believes: to the **Jew first,** and also to the Greek* (Gentile).

The 144,000 Jews represent the truly identifiable Jewish nation of Israel. It is they who must recognize Jesus as their Messiah, and due to the preaching of the two witnesses, and the powerful ensuing earthquake *Ch. 11:13,* they will begin to praise and glorify the God of heaven in this future scenario.

God first targeted His chosen people for redemption beginning with the faith of Abraham. Eventually, after many generations and centuries, the Jewish people rejected, and crucified their Messiah.

Because they rejected Jesus as their Savior and redeemer, the grace of God was spread abroad to the Gentiles.

Nevertheless, Romans 1:16 reminds us again that *the power of God is unto salvation to everyone that believes: to the **Jew first**, and also to the Greek* (Gentile).

When the earth is harvested, it might be that the 144,000 Jews must be presented to God, and approved by God **before** the Gentiles can be; because the Jews are the first fruits.

It might be that the main harvest of the earth, (The rapture of believers) composed primarily of Gentiles, cannot happen until the 144,000 Jews **(first fruits)** have accepted Jesus as their Messiah, and are presented to God the Father for His approval by Jesus Christ our high priest.

Lev.23: 9-11 says: *The Lord spoke to Moses saying, speak to the children of Israel, and say to them, when you come into the land which I give you, and shall reap the harvest, then you shall **bring a sheaf** (a bundle) of the **first fruits** of your harvest to the priest: and he shall "**wave**" the sheaf before the Lord, to be accepted for you.*

For health purposes a sample of the first fruits of the harvest had to be brought to the high priest for inspection. He would check it for obvious defects, and then wave it before the Lord to see if the Lord also approved of it. If so, then the okay was given to harvest the main crop.

There's an old time Christian hymn that's based on *Lev.23: 9-11* If you know it sing with me: *Bringing in the Sheaves, bringing in the Sheaves, we shall come rejoicing, bringing in the Sheaves. Bringing in the Sheaves, bringing in the Sheaves, we shall come rejoicing, bringing in the Sheaves.*

The 144,000 could be the *first fruits* of the harvest, just like the **"Wave offering"** was the first fruits without spot, or blemish, and without fault before the throne of God.

Therefore it might be that the main harvest of the earth, (The rapture of believers) composed primarily of Gentiles, **cannot** happen until the 144,000 Jews **(first fruits)** have accepted Jesus as their Messiah, (that's what makes them spotless, and without blemish), and are presented to God the Father for His approval by Jesus Christ our High Priest.

When the earth is harvested, it might be that the 144,000 Jews must be presented to God, and approved by God **before** the Gentiles can be. The question is: will the 144,000 be approved before God at that time? Rev.14: 3-5 answers that question.

Rev.14: 3-5 *The 144,000 Jews were redeemed from among men by the blood of the Lamb. In their mouth was found no guile, they were without fault before the throne of God.* **They passed inspection!**

*The 144,000 Jews might be the **first fruit** unto God,* just like the harvest sample was, but the church (the body of Christ) is the **main harvest.** The rapture of the church is comprised mostly of Gentiles.

When the 144,000 have accepted Jesus as their Messiah they will be presented to God, and approved by God, in this future scenario, then the main harvest (the rapture) of all other believers can happen.

Could it be that the divine harvest of the earth will be accomplished in the same three steps that the fields of Boaz were harvested in the book of Ruth?

Step # 1. The first fruits were presented by the high priest before God as a "Wave offering" for His approval *Lev.23: 9-11.* When the time comes for Jesus to harvest the earth, the 144,000 Jews (the first fruits) could be like that "Wave offering" sample.

Step # 2. After the 144,000 (first fruits) are approved, then approval is given to reap the main harvest. True believers in Jesus Christ worldwide, comprised mostly of Gentiles, will be the main harvest.

Step # 3. The gleaning of the four corners of the field. Leviticus 23: 22 says: *When you reap the harvest of your land, you shall not make a clean riddance of the corners of your field when you reap, neither shall you gather any gleaning of your harvest: you shall leave them for the poor, and to the stranger: I am the Lord your God.*

The survivors of the great tribulation, who **did not** receive the mark of the beast, might represent the four corners of the field (the world) left to be harvested. Many of them will be lead to the Lord (gleaned) by the redeemed priests of God who will reign with Jesus for 1000 years. That's us; and we will have our resurrected bodies at that time *Rev.20: 6.*

Just as Ruth worked in the field of Boaz, and gleaned the four corners after the main harvest; we as the bride of Christ will continue to work in the four corners of the earth to harvest as many souls as possible for our Lord and Savior during the millennial reign of Christ. Satan will be bound at that time.

But this is a future scenario. As of Rev.14: 12, the rapture of the saints has **not** yet occurred. There is still time for anyone who has **not** willingly taken the mark of the beast, to repent of their sins and ask Jesus Christ to come into their heart, and save their soul.

Because the Jews rejected Jesus, their Messiah, over 2000 years ago, God spread His grace abroad to the Gentiles. This time of grace in which we now live is called the church age. The church age will end with the fullness of the Gentiles Rom.11: 25, when the last Gentile that should be saved, is saved, just prior to ….. *The rapture of believers.*

REVELATION Chapter 14 B
The Harvest of the Earth is Ripe

First 3 ½ years of the tribulation

The Rapture Chapter

Rev.14: 14 *John sees one like the Son of man* (Jesus) *wearing a golden crown, and sitting* **on a cloud.** In the rapture Jesus meets us in the air. *In His hand He has a sharp sickle.* Sickles are used for harvesting.

Rev.14: 15-16 an angel cries with a loud voice "Thrust in thy sickle, and reap: for the time is come for thee to reap; for the harvest of the earth is ripe", and He thrust it in. This may be Jesus gathering to Himself the people of God.

I I Thess. 2: 1-2 *Now we beseech* (urge) *you brethren, by* **the coming of our Lord Jesus Christ, and by our gathering together unto Him** *that ye be not soon shaken in mind.*

This strongly implies the rapture of believers; when Jesus meets us in the air. The bible never actually uses the word rapture. Maybe a better word would be rescue, removal, or catching away, but they all imply the same thing. ~ **The rapid removal of believers!** ~

I Thess. 4: 16-17 tells us: *the Lord Himself shall descend from heaven with a shout, with the voice of the archangel, and with the trump of God: and the dead in Christ shall rise first: Then we which are alive and remain shall be caught up together with them in the clouds, to meet the Lord* **in the air:** *and so shall we ever be with the Lord.* **Jesus himself is the harvester.**

The dead in Christ is a huge number going back thousands of generations. The rapture is a gigantic resurrection; both of the dead, and of the living believers.

This is approximately the middle of the 7 years of the tribulation, just before the seventh seal is opened which begins the wrath of God on an unrepentant world. For 3 ½ years the antichrist has been forcing people to take the mark or die. He has broken the 7 year peace treaty with the Jews, killed the two witnesses, martyred millions of the saints of God, hijacked the temple, and exalted himself as God. *The anger of God is beyond hot at this time.*

This is likely to be the time when believers in Jesus Christ are removed from harms way, in a moment, in a twinkling of an eye, so that the Wrath of God can begin as the seventh seal is opened.

I Corin.15: 51-53 *Behold, I show you a mystery; we shall not all sleep, but we shall all be changed, in a moment, in a twinkling of an eye, at the last trump: for the trumpet shall sound, and the dead shall be raised incorruptible, and we shall be changed. For this corruptible must put on incorruption, and this mortal must put on immortality.*

Since it's appointed to every man once to die *Heb. 9:27*, it **might be** that when we are changed from mortals to immortals, we might actually die for an instant, as we are changed from mortals to immortals in a moment of time.

Verse 54, 55 *So when this corruptible shall have put on incorruption, and this mortal shall have put on immortality, then shall be brought to pass the saying that is written, Death is swallowed up in victory. O death, where is thy sting? O grave, where is thy victory?*

At that time believers will receive new immortal resurrected bodies, and the living saints of God will be taken out of harms way, as Jesus meets us in the air.

One might wonder why Jesus comes down to us, as we go up to Him. Perhaps it's for the same reason that the father in Luke 15:11-32 ran to meet his prodigal son when he saw him afar off. The father longed for his son's return; so when he saw him at a distance he ran to embrace him. The father then took him home, and prepared a great celebration feast for him, just as Jesus will do for us at the wedding feast of the Lamb.

Noah's family was removed from harms way just before the flood of God's judgment.

Lot's family was removed just before God judged Sodom and Gomorrah. Believers will be removed from harms way just before God's wrath is poured on this wicked world.

"Revelation 14: 14 thru 16" *The harvesting or gathering of the ripened earth by Jesus Christ himself* is seldom ever mentioned as a possible time for the rapture to occur, and yet the likelihood of it occurring at that time is very high, and very logical. What else could these verses be referring to, if not, Jesus gathering all believers (His bride) unto himself? At the rapture Jesus meets believers if the air, so this is **not** His second coming to the earth.

But this is a future scenario. It is logical to think the rapture will occur after the first 3 ½ years of worldwide preaching by the two witnesses, so that millions of new converts will be included in the rapture of believers.

~~~~~~

The Grapes of Wrath

Rev.14: 17 *another angel came out of the temple of heaven also having a sickle.* The first reaper with a sickle, which was Jesus, harvested good wheat (Believers) but the second reaper will harvest the grapes of wrath. (Unbelievers)

The harvest of the wicked begins immediately after the rapture of believers, and only **angels** are mentioned as harvesters. That's how we know these are two different harvestings, and not Jesus doing both of them.

Matt.13: 41-42 says: *the son of man shall **send forth his angels**, and **they shall gather** out of his kingdom all things that offend, and them that do iniquity; **and shall cast them into a furnace of fire:** there shall be wailing and gnashing of teeth.*

Rev.14: 17-20 another angel with a sickle is told to *"Gather the clusters of the vine of the earth, for her grapes are fully ripe, and cast them into the great wine press of the wrath of God."* These might be the grapes of wrath spoken of in *Joel 3:13*.

Joel 3: 13 *Put ye in the sickle, for the harvest is ripe: come, get you down; for the press is full, the fats overflow; for their wickedness is great.*

Not wine, but blood came from these grapes because these are the grapes of wrath. These are actual people who have blasphemed God, and rejected His grace and mercy time and time again. *And the winepress was trodden outside the city.* Where was Jesus crucified? Jesus was crucified outside of the city of Jerusalem.

They were given **one last chance to repent** just before the rapture occurred, as the angel in Rev.14: 6 *flew around the world preaching the everlasting gospel unto every nation, kindred, tongue, and people.* Many repented, many did not.

Rev.14: 6 is ahead of Rev.14:14-16 so the angel flew around the world preaching the gospel before the rapture occurred.

The Gospel will be preached around the world in three different ways as we draw near to the rapture.

#1. Christians are commanded to *"Go into all the world and preach the gospel to every creature" Mark 16:15.*

#2. God will send two powerful witnesses who will stand before all the earth to preach and prophecy for the first 3 ½ years of the tribulation *Rev.11: 3.*

#3. Just before the rapture, an angel will fly around the world preaching the everlasting gospel to every nation, kindred, tongue, and people *Rev.14: 6.*

What form this angel will take is uncertain, but all angels are ministering spirits, according to *Heb.1:1*. This powerful angel might minister the gospel to the hearts of men at this time of worldwide critical mass by *spiritually influencing* the inhabatance of the earth, as he circumnavigates the globe: In other words *"Strong personal conviction."*

God is not willing that any should parish. He goes to great lengths to save as many as possible. What a wonderful Savior He is.

So this is a different harvest, and different harvesters. Jesus harvested the, "good wheat" (believers), and the angels harvested the, "grapes of wrath" (unbelievers).

We've been studying the rapture of the church. *The purpose of the rapture is to remove believers from harms way* so God can exact revenge, and punishment on those who have harmed His people.

The rapture is the same thing as the first resurrection mentioned in Rev.20: 6. There is **no** difference. If there were a difference, then there would be two major resurrections happening almost back to back. It makes more sense that they are **not** two events, but one.

With the powerful preaching of the two anointed witnesses in chapter 11, isn't it more logical that God would simply wait 3 ½ more years to include all new converts?

Everything we have studied so far has happened in the first 3 ½ years of the tribulation. The second 3 ½ years are all contained in *Ch.8, 9 and 15-18*.

An interesting thing about our study of the first 3 ½ years of the tribulation is that two of the first 14 chapters don't seem to belong in the first 3 ½ years of the tribulation. They are Chapters 8 and 9. They clearly speak of the wrath of God which occurs in the second 3 ½ years.

I wouldn't change the content of the Bible for anything; but *for teaching purposes only* I would teach chapters 8 and 9 after chapter 14 so that all the chapters pertaining to the wrath of God would be kept together. See chart below

Rapture

First 3 ½ years = *tribulation.*   !   **Second 3 ½ years** = *Wrath of God.*
                                      !
Chapters 1 ----- 7 v 10 -----14 ! ^ Ch.15 -----18
                 v   ^
              Ch. 8, 9, _ _ _   ^

The first 3 ½ years of the 7 years of the tribulation is not the wrath of God, but the wrath of the antichrist poured out on all who oppose his *One World Order.* The **One World Order** is an evil world regime designed to destroy all opposition, and ultimately exalt Satan, through his right hand man (the antichrist) as king of all the kingdoms of this world. He is a counterfeit to Jesus Christ *"King of Kings and Lord of Lords."*

With the saints safely removed from harms way, God will *begin* to pour out His wrath in the last 3 ½ years of the great tribulation with the opening of the 7th seal. The 7th seal contains the 7 trumpets, and 7 bowls judgment, followed by the battle of Armageddon. This will be the harvesting of *the grapes of wrath*.

REVELATION Chapter 19 A
The Marriage Supper of the Lamb

Immediately after the rapture of believers is the *"Marriage Super of the Lamb."*

Let's take a close look at the bride of Christ, the body of believers, the *"true church"* as referenced in Eph.5: 23-27.

Eph.5: 25 *Christ loved the church and gave himself for it*. Believers are the church; the body of Christ. V: 23 says, *Jesus is the head of the church and the Savior of the body.*

The ultimate goal of Jesus is to present to *Himself*, this church that He paid such a heavy price for, and cared so much for by interceding for us throughout the ages.

Jesus sacrificed His own blood, and now He wants to present to *Himself* this pure and holy church without spot, wrinkle, or blemish. Jesus is constructing His own bride to His own perfection. What guy wouldn't want to be able to do that?

Folks, **we are** that church, **the bride** of Christ, and what is our part in preparing for this magnificent event? *Matt.22: 37-40 we must love the Lord with all our heart, soul, mind, and strength, and our neighbor as our selves.* We must live holy, sanctified lives that are pleasing to God.

Rev.19: 1-3 John hears **one great voice** *of many people in heaven praising God.* In this case "many people" means billions of resurrected saints. The harmony there is so perfect that they sound like one voice as they shout *"Alleluia: Salvation, and glory, and honor, and power unto the Lord our God"*. Did you know that in almost any language on earth, *"Alleluia"* means praise the Lord?

Rev.19: 4-5 *and the 24 elders, and the 4 beasts fell down, and worshiped God who sat on the throne.*

The 24 elders are likely to be the twelve sons of Jacob, whose name God changed to **Israel** back in the Old Testament *Gen.35:10-12*. The other 12 are likely to be the 12 New Testament disciples, making a total of 24 elders.

The 4 beasts are likely to be Seraphim angels. These very powerful elite angels are fewer in number than the Cherubim angels, and always seem to be in close proximity to the throne of God. *(Rev.4: 8, 9) (Isaiah 6: 2, 3)*

Rev.19: 6 this great multitude in heaven is comprised of everyone whose name is written in the Lambs book of life; all who have accepted Jesus' invitation to the wedding feast. They were included in the first resurrection of the dead (the rapture). The first resurrection is when these mortals will have received their immortal bodies. Their souls were already redeemed, but their bodies were still waiting to be redeemed. That happens at the first resurrection of the dead; (which is the same as the rapture).

Rev.19: 7 you can feel the excitement building as they say *"Let us be glad, and rejoice, and give honor to Him: for the marriage of the Lamb is come, and His wife has made herself ready."* Now we see what the excitement is all about; the marriage of the Lamb and His bride is about to be celebrated in all of its glory.

Rev.19: 8 *the bride is **given** the cleanest, whitest, finest linen that heaven can provide because it represents righteousness.* Faithful believers are the bride of Christ. We do **not** come to Jesus with our own righteousness. It is given to us by Him.

Rev.19: 9 *blessed indeed are they who are called to the marriage supper of the Lamb.* They are not the guests, but the bride of Christ. They have answered the call of God.

Rev.19: 10 Overwhelmed at the thought of being called unto the marriage supper of the Lamb, *John falls at the feet of the angel to worship him,* but the angel says "Do not do it I am a fellow servant (a created being), worship God."

At this point in this future scenario, we can assume that the wedding celebration has taken place. From now on, wherever the groom is, the bride will also be.

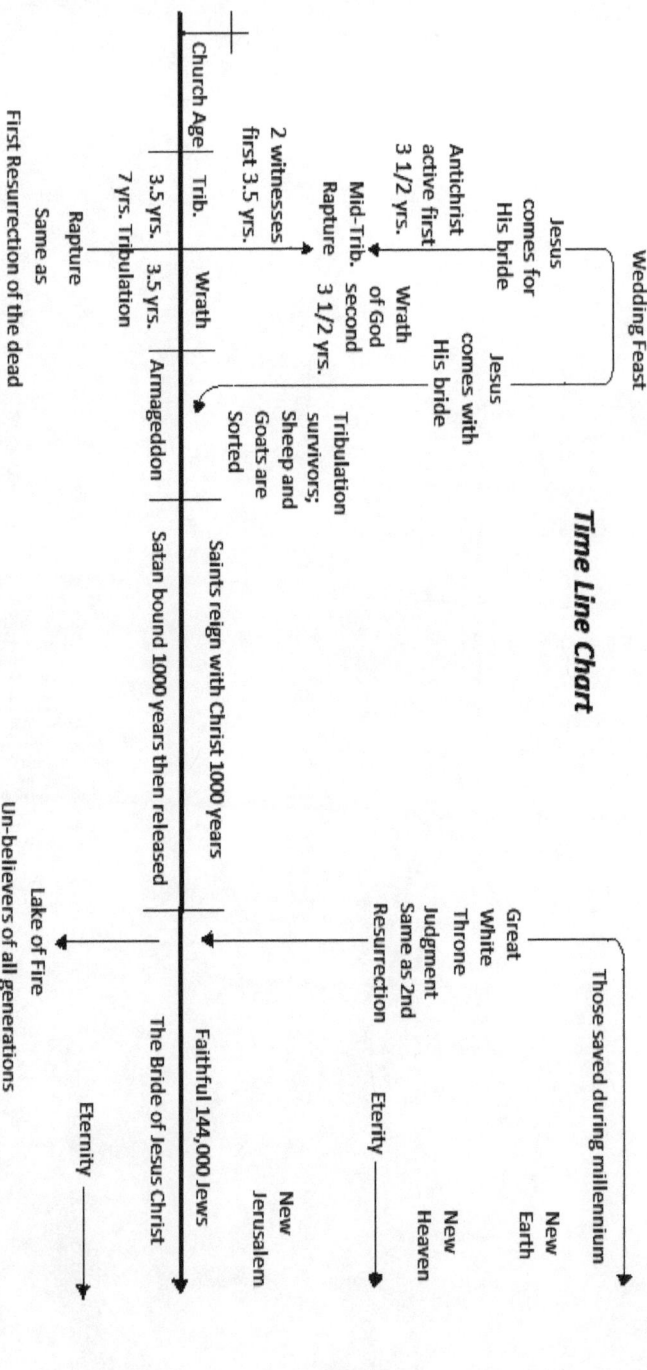

~Part Two~

Second 3 ½ Years of Seven Year Tribulation
THE WRATH OF GOD

REVELATION Chapter 8

Seventh Seal Opened

Seven Trumpets Sound **The Wrath of God begins**

God is about to disassemble the 10 kingdom coalition that antichrist has set up to make himself king of all the kingdoms of this world.

The first 6 seals of judgment occur in the first 3 ½ years. The seventh, which is the last seal of judgment, occurs in the second 3 ½ years of the tribulation.

The 7th seal unleashes two more series of seven judgments, the trumpets, and the bowls.

No trace of **Gentile Christians** will be found on earth during the last 3 ½ years of the tribulation. *(Chapters 8, 9, 15, 16, 17, 18)* God has mercifully removed them (via the rapture) out of harms way (At approximately mid- tribulation), just before God's wrath comes down on *those left behind.*

Keep in mind that Christians are **not** subject to the wrath of God, because we are at peace with God. *Rom.5: 9, Rom.8:1, and I Thess. 5: 9*

Genesis Ch.18 Abraham asked the angel if God would spare the city of Sodom if there were 50 righteous people there, and the angel said "yes". Then he asked about 45, 30, 20, and 10, but what if he would have gone down to one? Do you think God would have spared Sodom for the sake of just *one* righteous person?

The answer is "yes", so God had to remove, or protect every last one of them, because God's people are not subject to the wrath of God.

Christians **are** subject to tribulation. Even Jesus said *"In this world you will have tribulation; but be of good cheer, I have overcome the world." John 16:33*

Christians **are** present during the first 3 ½ years of the tribulation. How else could the antichrist make war with them, and overcome them? *Rev.13: 7*

Now our study of the first 3 ½ years is finished, and we are about to begin our study of the second 3 ½ years. Revelation is **not** necessarily written in chronological order.

To begin the second 3 ½ years we must go to chapters *8, 9, and* then *15-18*

Rev.8: 1 *when the Lamb of God opened the 7th seal, there was silence in heaven for about a half of an hour.* Why?

This is a very somber and sobering moment of time to assess the devastation, terror, and horrible judgment that is about to begin on the rebellious reprobates *left behind* on earth. This is not a time of salvation, rehabilitation, restoration, or regeneration. This is the time of God's **undiluted wrath** on those who have already made their decision to reject the grace and mercy of Jesus Christ. God is no longer interested in saving these people. They have already closed their minds and hardened their hearts. Their conscience has been seared with a hot iron.

Rev.8: 2-3 *John sees seven angels standing before God holding seven trumpets, and before any of them begin to blow, another angel stood at the altar of God having a golden censer.*

This angel was given much incense (Sweet fragrance) to offer with the prayers of the saints on the altar which was before the throne of God. God remembers the prayers of the saints throughout the generations as they pleaded for God's justice and revenge. Perhaps the incense implies that this will be "sweet revenge".

Rev.8: 5 *the angel filled the censer (measuring device) with fire from the altar, and cast it into the earth.*

Rev.8: 6-7 *the **first trumpet** was blown and there was **hail and fire, mingled with blood**, cast upon the earth and **1/3 of the trees** and grass were burned up.*

Rev.12: 12-14 Tell us the woman (Israel, and the 144,000 believing Jews) still on earth after the rapture of the saints are protected for the last 3 ½ years of the great tribulation while God brings His undiluted wrath on this wretched world. All Gentile believers will have already been removed at that time via the rapture.

Rev.8: 8-9 *The second trumpet sounded and "a" great mountain burning with fire was cast into the sea and 1/3 of the sea became blood, 1/3 of sea life died, and 1/3 of the ships were destroyed.*

A great mountain burning sounds like it could be an active volcano, but it's not likely that this is a volcano that blew its top, because the massive destruction spoken of here (1/3 of the sea) is more than any **one** volcano could produce. (Earth's surface is more than 3/5 water)

Something the size of a mountain falling from the sky, and being on fire could be an asteroid, or meteor from outer space, **or** possibly a fire brand from the prayer altar that is before the throne of God. Nothing like that is on the scientific radar at this time.

Rev.8: 10-11 *the third trumpet sounded and there fell a* **great burning star** *from heaven named "Wormwood".* **It made 1/3 of the fresh water bitter.** *Many people died due to the bitter water.* "Wormwood" means bitterness.

Here again we have **fire falling down from heaven**. This fire may have originated straight from the altar of the prayers of the saints who were martyred *Rev.8:5.*

Romans 12: 19-20 says *"Avenge not yourselves, but rather give place to wrath: for it is written, vengeance is mine; I will repay, says the Lord." If your enemy hungers, feed him, if he thirst, give him to drink; for in so doing you will heap coals of fire on his head.............* It's very possible that ***these are those coals!***

Rev.8: 12 the *fourth trumpet* sounded and **one third of the sun, moon, stars, and earth were darkened.** A celestial phenomenon is happening.

The size of the sun in relation to the earth is like a basketball beside a garden pea. They are 93,000,000 miles apart. What would it take to darken the sun alone by one third?

One third of the sun could be darkened if one third of the light were somehow blocked from reaching the earth. (That could happen)

To block one third of the light of the sun, moon, and stars from reaching the earth there would have to be something massive happening in the celestial heavens; such as a thick cloud of meteors or asteroid like objects between the sun and the earth.

Some would have to be large enough to look like a burning mountain as it fell into the sea, and destroyed one third of the marine life. This would be consistent with the second trumpet judgment.

If there were enough of them coming toward the earth they could reduce the light of the sun, moon, stars, and the amount of sunshine on earth by one third.

Most of them would no doubt miss the earth, or burn up in the earth's atmosphere, but plenty of them would hit, and cause great devastation.

The source of these fire brands could be a celestial phenomenon, **or** they could come straight from the prayer altar that is before the throne of God. It contains the prayers of the saints that have been martyred as well as other saints who have been wronged.

Think how terrifying it will be in the day of God's wrath when people can be hit at any time, day or night by something big or small entering from outer space.

Believers don't have to worry about this, because we are at peace with God. We will have been removed from harms way via the rapture before God's wrath begins.

But why would there even be an altar in heaven? Typically an altar is a place where animals were killed, and sacrificed. Why would sacrifices be necessary in heaven?

Sacrifices would **not** need to be made in heaven. These sacrifices were already made on earth by these saints who had been persecuted throughout the ages. But their prayers for God to avenge their enemies are stored up against the day of God's wrath. They are stored in the altar that is before the throne of God.

REVELATION Chapter 9

Demons from Bottomless Pit, and Euphrates River

Last 3 ½ years **The Wrath of God**

Rev.9: 1 *The fifth trumpet sounded and John sees a **star** fall from heaven to earth, and to **him** was given the key to the bottomless pit.* (The Abyss)

We know that the **star** was a person by the personal pronoun **"him"**. Satan is described as a falling star Luke 10:18. Jesus said *"I beheld Satan as lightning fall from heaven."*

Rev.9: 2 *Satan opened the bottomless pit and smoke came out **like** the smoke of a great furnace, enough to darken the sun, and the sky.* (Like millions of bats out of a cave)

Rev.9: 3-4 Out *of the smoke came locusts. The locusts were told **not** to hurt any green thing, only those men who had **not** the seal of God in their forehead.* Who would that include? Jews: no, their already marked in their foreheads. Christians: no, their gone via the rapture. So who is left? Only the wicked and rebellious people who missed the rapture are left. Most of them have taken the mark of the beast, but not all; some of them actually opposed the antichrist even though they missed the rapture as unbelievers.

Locust (insects) could not make the distinction between green plants and humans, but demons could. These are obviously **not** normal locusts that eat every green thing in sight. They are very likely to be demons from the pit of hell.

These demons are forbidden to hurt anyone who has the seal of God in their forehead. Rev.7: 3-4 informed us that 12,000 Jews were sealed in their foreheads from each of the twelve tribes of Israel. This would imply that these 144,000 Jews are still on earth after the rapture of the church, but they are being protected by God.

We are **now** studying the second 3 ½ years of the tribulation. No trace of the believing *Gentile* church can be found on earth in chapters 8 or 9, because they are safely with the Lord in heaven. Yet the 144,000 Jewish believers are still present on the earth.

By God's design, the 144,000 may have missed the rapture because Gentile believers are God's spiritually chosen people, while the Jews are God's earthly chosen people. It might be that God has left the 144,000 faithful Jews on earth during the last 3 ½ years of the great tribulation because of Matt. 24:22 which says: *and except those days should be shortened, there should no flesh be saved: but for the elect's sake those days shall be shortened.*

The 144,000 are the elect of God who will remain on earth to prevent God's wrath from destroying all flesh. If all flesh were destroyed by the wrath of God; then He could **not** fulfill His prophecies and promises to the Jews in the millennium.

I doubt that the 144,000 Jewish believers remain on earth to witness to the whole world, as many say they will, because in the first 3 ½ years they are **not** saved, and have accepted the antichrist as their Messiah with whom they have signed a peace treaty. However, we must give credit to the two Jewish witnesses in Chapter 11 for evangelizing the whole world in the first 3 ½ years of the tribulation.

When the antichrist killed the two witnesses, and hijacked their newly finished temple the Jews realize that they have been deceived by the antichrist, and are forced to flee into a wilderness hideout were God protects and nourishes them for the last 3 ½ years of the great tribulation. *Rev.12: 6, Matt.24:15-22.*

They will probably flee to a complex network of nuclear bomb shelters already built and well supplied deep under the mountains of Israel. So, the believing Jews will **not** be evangelizing the world during the last 31/2 years.

Rev.9: 5-6 God has allowed Satan to release these hideous demons to mercilessly torment those who showed no mercy to their fellow man.

Matt.5: 7 *"Blessed are the merciful for they shall be shown mercy."* The opposite is also true. Cursed are the merciless for they shall be shown **no** mercy.

God shows these people **no** mercy, they desire to die, and death flees from them. Perhaps these are the people responsible for the deaths of those martyrs under the altar. *Rev.6: 9-10*

Rev.9: 7-10 the description of these demons is both detailed and vague. Perhaps that is because demons (sometimes called devils) come in such a wide variety into the lives of mankind.

Getting into the description of these demons is probably not necessary. It suffices that they are evil angels. Clearly they are battle hardened warriors that we must never underestimate.

Eph.6: 12 says *"We wrestle not against flesh and blood, but against principalities, against powers, against the rulers of the darkness of this world, and against spiritual wickedness in high places."*

The way to oppose demons and devils is to rebuke them by the word of God, bind them in the name of Jesus, *resist them and they will flee from you. James 4: 7*

Rev.9:11 the fact that they have a king could imply that they have a rank and file system. They are well organized and have "a chain of command".

Rev.9: 13-15 *the* **sixth trumpet** *sounds and the angel is told to loose the four angels that are bound in the river Euphrates.*

Four angels were loosed which were prepared for an exact moment in time. In reverse order: (a year, a month, a day, an hour) to slay 1/3 of the earth's population. The timing on the slaughter of **one third** of earth's population is so exact that it's likely to be a nuclear exchange happening in diverse places around the world; in other words, a third world war. *Zechariah 14:12*

Zechariah 14: 12b *their flesh shall consume away <u>while they stand upon their feet</u>, and their eyes shall consume away in their holes, and their tongue shall consume away in their mouth.*

Believers should not be frightened by this because; God will have already removed them from harms way via the rapture. *Rev.14: 14-16*

Rev.9: 16 *the huge number of this army of horsemen (200,000,000)* tells us that in a day of modern warfare, actual horsemen would not be used, or capable of killing one third of the people of the earth. These are more likely to be another batch of demons.

These Euphrates River demons are a more deadly batch than the bottomless pit demons we spoke of earlier. This might be how we got the Greek word pandemonium. Pan: meaning "all" and demonian meaning "demonic"; thus pandemonium. God is allowing all the demons of hell to be released to torment and kill people in His wrath.

Rev.9: 20-21 *the rest of the people who were not killed by these plagues repented not*. They displayed no remorse, regret, or repentance for anything they have said or done. They are truly diabolical reprobates.

Chapter 15 is next in the order of events in the last 3 ½ years of the great tribulation.

REVELATION Chapter 15
Prelude to Seven Bowls Judgment

Last 3 ½ Years of the tribulation

Six of the seven trumpets have sounded

Rev.15: 1-2 *John sees a marvelous sign in heaven; seven angels having the last seven plagues. These bowls are filled with the wrath of God.*

He also sees a sea of glass which we learned earlier was before the throne of God. John described it as being clear as crystal. *Rev.4: 6*

However, *now it is mixed with fire.* Perhaps it is reflecting God's fury at this time. Remember, in our study, this is the time of God's wrath upon the wicked.

John also sees the martyrs that had gotten the victory over the beast, his image, his mark, and over the number of his name. How can a person be murdered by the antichrist and still be victorious?

They have the victory because *they did not serve the beast, or worship his image, or receive his mark,* and because they will experience eternal life with Jesus Christ their Savior.

Rev.15: 3-4 *they were standing on the sea of glass, and each had a harp. They were inspired to sing the song of Moses, and the song of the Lamb.*

The song of Moses is in *Exodus 15: 1-18*. It is a song of **glorious triumph** over their enemies, and the faithful deliverance by the Lord from the bondage of Egypt. The lyrics are that of worship: they were singing great and marvelous are your works, just and true are your ways, Oh King of saints.

Rev.15: 5-7 *the seven angels came out of the temple **holding the seven plagues***. Do you remember who the four beasts are? We learned earlier that they are Seraphim angels. *One of these 4 Seraphim gave unto the seven angels, seven golden bowls filled with the wrath of God.*

Rev.15: 8 *the temple was filled with smoke from the glory of God and from His power.*

God's anger is beyond hot at this time. He is filled with righteous indignation toward those who have shaken their puny fist in God's face, and blasphemed His Holy name.

He has been patient and long suffering. He has been kind and sacrificial, even giving up His life on a cruel cross. He has used every method available to seek and to save as many as possible. But this is an evil and adulteress generation, a generation of vipers. What more could God do than what He has already done to save as many as possible?

REVELATION Chapter 16

Seven Bowls Judgment

Last 3 ½ years of the tribulation

Undiluted Wrath of God

Rev.16: 1 John hears a great voice out of the temple saying to the seven angels *"Go your ways, pour out the bowls of the wrath of God upon the earth."*

The voice John heard from the temple could only be that of God Himself, because the last verse of the last chapter said *"no one else was allowed to be in the temple of God until the seven plagues were fulfilled."* That is: until God's anger is satisfied *Rev.15: 8*. God is continuing to systematically disassemble the 10 kingdom coalition that the un-holy trinity has set up.

Rev.16: 2 *the first angel poured out his bowl and there were ugly, **painful sores** on those who had the mark of the beast and worshiped his image.* It's almost as if they were marked in their foreheads for destruction; while the 144,000 Jews were marked in their foreheads for preservation. *Ch.7*

In this study there are three people groups on earth at this time: 1. those who have willingly taken the mark of the beast. 2. The 144,000 Jews marked by God in their foreheads. 3. Those that missed the rapture, but have **not** taken the mark of the beast.

Rev.16: 3 *the second angel poured out his bowl upon the **sea** and it became as the blood of a dead man. Every living thing in the salt water sea died.* Next is the fresh water.

Rev.16: 4 *the **third** angel poured out his **bowl** on the **rivers** and **springs** and they **became blood**.* Even the lakes and ground water would soon be polluted. That doesn't leave very much fresh drinking water.

Rev.16: 5-7 John hears the angel in charge of the waters say *"You are righteous Lord, because of your judgments, they have shed the blood of saints and prophets and you have given them blood to drink."*

What goes around comes around. They were cruel and blood thirsty people; so now, blood is just about all they have to drink. There's a parallel passage in *Isaiah 49:26*.

Isaiah 49: 26 says *"I will feed them that oppress thee (God's people) with their own flesh; and they shall be drunken with their own blood, as with sweet wine: and all flesh shall know that I the Lord am thy Savior and thy Redeemer, the mighty One of Jacob."*

A person can only live a few days without water, so we must assume that there is an available source of water. What do you suppose will be their only real source of drinking water during the second 3 ½ years of the tribulation?

In our study of Rev.11: 6, the two witnesses from God were given power to shut heaven that it rain **not** in the days of their prophecy. The days of their prophecy were the **first** 3 ½ years. So, in the first 3 ½ years of the tribulation there will probably be a worldwide drought. People will be fighting for water "rights" during that time. This may be one more reason for wars and rumors of wars to occur at that time.

If it rained not, or the rain was limited the **first** 3 ½ years of the 7 years of tribulation, then it's likely there will be more than enough rain the **second** 3 ½ years to sustain life. So, rain will probably be their only source of drinking water. It will probably be moderate and constant rather than heavy rain, because in 3 ½ years heavy rain would cause a worldwide flood.

Rev.14: 20 *says the winepress was trodden without the city, and blood came out of the wine press, even unto the horse's bridles, by the space of a thousand and six hundred furlongs;* which is about 180 miles at a depth of 4 ½ feet. Can you imagine this?

Most people think this happens at Armageddon; but I don't think so. I don't know where it actually happens but it probably happens **before**

Armageddon. With the seas, rivers, and streams turning to blood in *Rev.16: 3, 4*; plus this enormous amount of rainfall in the second 3 ½ years, it's easy to see how this blood, and water *mixture* could reach the level of a horse's bridle in some areas for 180 miles.

This blood isn't coming from dead people, but from rivers and streams that have been turned into blood, and then mixed with high volumes of rain water.

It probably happens **before** Armageddon because the heavy rainfall will stop **before** Armageddon starts. We know this because of the next bowl judgment.

Rev.16: 8-9 *the forth angel poured out his **bowl upon the sun** and fire was given to him to **scorch men with fire**.* Undoubtedly the rains will have stopped at this time. The sun is out, and it is hot! This could be a result of solar flares.

Even while being scorched with great heat, which no doubt causes them to have heat strokes, and blisters, they blaspheme the name of God who had power over the plagues.

Rev.16: 10-11 *the fifth angel poured out his **bowl** on **the throne of the beast** and his kingdom was **full of darkness**. They gnawed their tongues for pain.* Very little of the world's electrical grid will be operable at this time of world devastation and solar flares.

John 3:19 says this: *and this is the condemnation, that light is come into the world, and men loved darkness rather than light, because their deeds were evil.* Those who loved darkness more than light will get more darkness than they bargained for.

Rev.16: 12 *the sixth angel poured out his **bowl** on the river **Euphrates** and the water was **dried up** that the way of the kings of the east might be prepared.* The Euphrates River will probably be a mixture of blood and water at that time, but it will still dry up. The Euphrates River is a natural barrier to any ground attack from the east against Israel. The sixth bowl judgment would provide a dried up river bed by which huge armies could move westward to attack Israel. These would be land forces attacking from the east.

That seems like primitive combat for this day of modern warfare, but keep in mind that all of this happens after the world has been absolutely devastated by the 7 seals, 7 trumpets, and the 7 bowls, not to mention a possible nuclear war. *See: Zech.14:12*

What is happening is that God is gathering the 10 king coalition and their armies to fight this huge battle of Armageddon. This huge 10 kingdom coalition headed up by the "unholy trinity" (Satan, antichrist, and the false prophet) who will attempt to eliminate the Jewish people once and for all. They will think of it as *"The final solution."*

Obviously the Jew's hideout has been discovered by the antichrist and the 10 kingdom coalition. Believing Jews have been fed and protected by God for 3 ½ years; probably in nuclear fall out shelters under the mountains of Israel. By this time their supplies are depleted. They will have to emerge from their hideout.

The goal of the 10 kingdom coalition is to drive Israel into the Mediterranean Sea by attacking from the east, crossing the dried up Euphrates River, and moving westward.

Satan's ultimate goal is to eliminate the Jewish people so that God will never be able to fulfill that most important unfulfilled Old Testament prophecy. **Ezekiel 37: 27-28** *my tabernacle also shall be with them: Yea, I will be their God, and they shall be my people. And the heathen shall know that I the Lord do sanctify Israel, when my sanctuary shall be in the midst of them for evermore.*

Isaiah 55:11 God says *"So shall my word be that goes forth out of my mouth: it shall not return unto me void, but it shall accomplish that which I please, and it shall prosper in the thing whereto I sent it."*

Satan knows that if he can keep God from fulfilling that prophecy, he has made God a liar like himself. God would no longer have the legal ability to condemn him to the lake of fire where he will be tormented day and night forever. *Rev.20:10*

In this future scenario the Jews are no longer deceived as to whom their true Messiah is. Now Satan must make one last all-out effort to destroy them at the battle of Armageddon. The 144,000 believing Jews must be present on the earth during the battle of Armageddon for that to happen. The fact is, it will **not** happen because in Ch.19, God will prevent Satan's plan.

Rev.16: 13-14 John sees *three unclean spirits like frogs come out of the mouths of the dragon (Satan), the beast (antichrist), and the false prophet* (antichrist's spokesman).

These three are the unholy trinity. Why the unclean spirits are like frogs is uncertain, but ask yourself what is the most predominate feature of a frog in relation to the rest of its body? It is its mouth. The unclean spirit of devils is coming from these **three big mouths**.

They are the spirits of devils working miracles (Such as calling down fire from heaven *Rev.13:13.)*

Perhaps these three big mouths are trying to rally any militant force in the world who will listen; to be involved in a unilateral attack on Israel. The purpose is to gather them to the battle of Armageddon.

Obviously the hiding place of the 144,000 Jews has been discovered by this time, and the unholy trinity wants to use what's left of the 10 kingdom coalition to unilaterally attack, and destroy Israel at Armageddon.

Rev.16: 15 Jesus himself interjects to say, *"Behold, I come as a thief. Blessed is **he** that is watching and keeps **his** garment, (of righteousness) lest **he** walk naked, and **they** see **his** shame."* To whom is Jesus speaking? It's likely that Jesus' statement at this time is directed strictly to the remnant of Jews (the 144,000) as encouragement for them to keep their faith intact to the very end.

They will have been discovered by the antichrist by then. Jesus will come quickly (like a thief in the night) to rescue them from total annihilation at the battle of Armageddon. Jesus is **not** addressing Gentile believers because they have been removed via the rapture.

Matt.24: 21-22 *"There shall be great tribulation such as was **not** since the beginning of the world to this time, no, nor ever shall be. And except those days be shortened, there should no flesh be saved: but for the **elect's** sake, those days will be shortened."*

The **elect** of God are the 144,000 Jews; the only Christians still on earth at this time. Were it not for their presence, it's likely that no flesh would survive the undiluted wrath of God.

We can know the Jews are still present on the earth during the 7 bowls judgment because their homeland is about to be attacked by the unholy trinity, *and a huge global coalition of 10 kings with their armies at Armageddon.* *Rev.16: 13-14*

Please notice the last line of Rev.16: 14. The battle is identified as *"that Great Day of God Almighty."* This battle belongs to the Lord, not to the spirit of devils; and not to the spirit of those *"three big mouths."*

Rev.16: 16 The KJV says *"He"* (God Almighty) *gathered them to a place called in Hebrew, Armageddon.* They think they gathered themselves there to destroy Israel. Actually it is God gathering these kings and their armies to Armageddon for their own destruction. This chapter does not describe the actual battle. That battle is best described in chapter 19.

Rev.16: 17-18 *the **seventh** angel poured out his **bowl** into the air and out of the temple of heaven came a great voice from the throne of God saying "IT IS DONE".*

What is done? The 7 seals, 7 trumpets, and now the last of the 7 bowls judgment are all poured out.

This 7th bowl judgment poured into the air will send a message to the world that God is still in control. Even at this point of total devastation around the world, **God is Almighty.**

The 7th bowl judgment will also include lightning, rumbling, thunder, and a worldwide earthquake *much larger than any before.* This enormous earthquake, unlike the one in Revelation Chapter 6, **is** part of the wrath of God. This powerful earthquake might be the one that causes the earth to reel to and fro like a drunkard as mentioned in *Isaiah 24: 20.* The earth will literally wobble on its axis.

REVELATION Chapter 17 A
Mystery Babylon

Last 3 ½ years of the tribulation **The Wrath of God**

Rev.17: 1-2 *One of the seven powerful angels that had the seven bowls offers to show John the judgment of the great harlot that sits on many waters.* The seven bowls have already been poured out, so we must assume that **we are looking back on earlier events.**

Mystery Babylon, the great harlot is probably the chief city of the dragon and the antichrist's evil world regime. It is probably the capital of the corrupt world system that viciously martyrs God's people. We are looking back on the capital city "Mystery Babylon" that existed until the seven bowls were poured out.

Rev.17: 3 *John is carried away "in the spirit"* (a spiritual state in which one receives divine revelation.) *John was carried into the wilderness;* (a spiritually desolate place). *He sees a woman sitting upon a scarlet beast which is supporting and carrying her. The beast is full of names of blasphemy. This scarlet colored, blasphemous beast the woman is riding on has 7 heads and 10 horns,* like the antichrist in Rev.13: 1.

The horns refer to kings or kingdoms according to *Rev.17: 12* which says: *the ten horns which you saw are ten kings, which have received no kingdom as yet; but receive power as kings* **one hour** *with the beast.* That's when the antichrist appointed them kings over the 10 kingdoms of the world.

This sounds like they are **not** kings chosen by their countrymen, but czars appointed by this world dictator. So the antichrist is the beast with 7 heads and 10 horns. He heads up the coalition of 10 kings that support the wicked city, the great harlot. She is probably supported with tax monies from the 10 kingdom coalition. That could be a lot of revenue for one city.

This coalition is comprised of 10 kingdoms. Each kingdom will be composed of many countries. Each king will answer to the antichrist as if he is the king of kings.

Dan.7: 8 *Daniel considered the horns and behold there came up among them another little horn before whom there were three of the first horns plucked up by the roots: and behold in this horn were eyes like the eyes of a man, and a mouth speaking great things.*

The little horn **is** the antichrist that plucked up 3 of the first 10 horns (kings) temporarily reducing their total to 7 kings. However, Rev.17:12-14 implies that the three kings who were plucked up will be replaced, to bring the total back up to ten before the battle of Armageddon begins.

The 3 kings were probably removed due to a lack of full compliance to the antichrist's One World agenda. But they have been replaced by 3 kings who will comply.

So the 10 kings will unilaterally agree to attack Israel. This battle will take place at Armageddon. But keep in mind that the actual battle of Armageddon occurs in chapter 19; though it's mentioned in chapters 16 and 17.

Now let's take a look at Mystery Babylon before she was destroyed by God's wrath.

Rev.17:5 This wicked city has *a name written on her forehead, MYSTERY BABYLON, MOTHER OF HARLETS, and ABOMINATIONS OF THE EARTH.*

Cities don't have foreheads, but they do have reputations, and this title is her legacy. We can assume that the kingdom of the antichrist will have a headquarter city that will be revealed at that time. It may go by a different name than Babylon, but it will be the same wicked city. It will probably be the headquarters of the antichrist, and will probably be located somewhere within the former Roman Empire.

Rev.17: 6 *John is mesmerized by the sight of the woman, drunk on the blood of the saints, and the martyrs who remained faithful unto death.* How could she be so cold and cruel? The fact is that more Christians have been martyred in the 20th century than in all of the previous 19 centuries combined.

Rev.17: 7 *the angel in John's heavenly vision offers to tell him the mystery of the woman* (Mystery Babylon) *and the beast* (antichrist's world regime) *with 7 heads and 10 horns, on which she rides.* Another name for the 10 kingdom coalition could be the Revived Roman Empire.

So Mystery Babylon (The headquarter city) is riding on (supported by) the antichrist's world regime which is the 10 kingdom coalition. In other words, the Revived Roman Empire will financially support Mystery Babylon. So the antichrist is using the Revived Roman Empire to get what he really wants; ***A One World Empire of his own.***

Rev.17: 8 The mystery of Mystery Babylon is that the beast (the revived Roman Empire) carrying the woman (Mystery Babylon) "**was** (past), **is not** (present), **and yet is** (a future coming), **and shall ascend out of the bottomless pit,** (hell) **for a short time, and then go into perdition** (Doom)." Satan is going to revive the old Roman Empire on a worldwide scale for a short time.

If indeed this beast is the antichrist, **or** part of the One World System that he heads up; then we can speculate as to **what world system "was, is not, and yet is."**

Rev.17: 9 historically, ancient Rome **"was"** famous for being situated on seven hills. Rome **was** the capital of the Roman Empire, and had a world system that persecuted Christians and Jews at that time.

It would seem that **the Roman Empire** has not existed for many centuries. However, if it does exist in a dormant state, waiting for an opportune time to rise up again, then the old Roman Empire would be a world empire that **"was, is not, and yet is."**

The Roman Empire was (in Jesus' days), **is not** (for many centuries, including now), **and yet is** (poised to rise again in the end times) headed up by the antichrist and his coalition of ten evil kings. Keep in mind that the Roman Empire has never been over thrown; so it could still exist.

Ten evil kings who rule over 10 kingdoms around the world are all core groups loyal to the antichrist, and strongly opposed to anyone who did **not** take the mark of the beast. They are more than willing to "rid the world" of those who refuse to take the mark of the beast, and be part of the new One World Order. The *"One World Order"* of the antichrist is a counter balance to the *"One World Order"* of the millennial reign of Jesus Christ.

All of these are part of the same system: Mystery Babylon, the Harlot, the 10 kingdom coalition, the Global Agenda of the antichrist, and the Revived Roman Empire are all the same system that will be headed up by the antichrist as he attempts to form his own ***"One World Order"*** with him as king of all kings.

All this is what led up to the wrath of God, and the destruction of Mystery Babylon. It will all culminate at the battle of Armageddon.

REVELATION Chapter 17 B
Mystery Babylon Continued

Last 3 ½ years of the tribulation **The Wrath of God**

Rev.17: 9 says: *Here is the mind that has wisdom;* giving us fair warning that what is coming up in the next few verses is very challenging.

Rev.17: 10-11 say this: *There are seven kings: **five are fallen**, and **one is**, and **the other is not yet come**; and when he comes, he must continue a short space. And the beast that was, and is not, even he is the eighth, and is of the seven, and goes into perdition* (doom).

So, Rev.17:10-11 speak of the 7 kingdoms (empires), of which 5 are fallen.

What Five world empires do we know of historically that have fallen? 1. Ancient Egypt 2. Assyria 3. Babylon 4. Media-Persia, and 5. Greece. These are five world empires that have fallen.

The next world empire (the sixth) **"is"**; current to John's time.

In John's day that could only be … the Roman Empire by which he was being persecuted, and exiled to the island of Patmos.

The (seventh world empire), as of John's time, has **"not yet come"** implying that it is in the process of coming. The question is: Could it be the **revived** Roman Empire mentioned in Rev.17: 8 that *was, is not, and yet is?*

So if the 6th world empire is the Roman Empire, then the 7th is likely to be the Revived Roman Empire. Keep in mind that the Roman Empire has never been over thrown; so it could still exist.

The Roman Empire was (in Jesus' days), **is not** (for many centuries, including now), **and yet is** (poised to rise again during the tribulation) headed up by the antichrist.

Rev.17: 11 tells us that, *there is an eighth world empire.* The eighth could be "Mystery Babylon", possibly headquartered in Europe, and headed up by the antichrist, and still be part of the seventh. The seventh empire being the revived Roman Empire.

Rev.17: 12-15 *Ten independent rulers, of the 10 kingdom coalition, who have been loyal to the antichrist, will meet with him briefly (one hour). They will unite with one mind, joining forces, and giving their power and strength to the beast.* Antichrist will then give them their marching orders. **Destroy Israel!**

Although the Roman Empire was considered a world empire it was limited primarily to Europe, but the scope and range of the Revived Roman Empire will be worldwide. Therefore the Revived Roman Empire should be counted as a separate world empire.

The seventh and eight world empires will be blended until the antichrist highjacks the newly built temple, and declares himself to be God *II Thess.2: 4*. The antichrist will use the Revived Roman Empire to reveal himself to the world, but he will build his own brand new **One World Order; "Mystery Babylon"**, not belonging to Julius Caesar, but to the antichrist himself. It could be the eighth world empire.

It would seem that the three kings, who had been uprooted by the antichrist, must have been replaced by three kings who will be more compliant to him, because the number of kings is back up from 7 to 10.

This reconstituted coalition of 10 kings will cross the dried up Euphrates River, moving westward to fight the final battle of Armageddon, designed to drive Israel into the Mediterranean Sea. Excluded from the "rapture" by God's design; believing Israel must still be on earth for this attack on their homeland to happen.

This could be Satan's last chance to destroy the Jews, and to prevent God's most important unfulfilled prophecies. Ezekiel 37: 27-28 *my tabernacle also shall be with them: yea, "I will be their God and they shall be my people. And the heathen shall know that I the Lord do sanctify Israel, when my sanctuary shall be in the midst of them forevermore.* Israel is saved at this time in the future, but Jesus is not yet dwelling in the midst of them; that will happen in the millennium.

If Satan could prove God a liar by destroying the Jewish nation at Armageddon then God could **not** legally condemn him to the lake of fire, where he will be tormented day and night forever and ever *Rev.20:10*. The lake of fire is Satan's worst fear.

The harlot (Mystery Babylon) is sitting on the backs of, and at the expense of the various nations of the world. This wicked city has been extremely corrupt, arrogant, hoity, and self-serving. There is dissension in the ranks, and danger in the air.

Verses 16 and 17 *say the beast and the 10 horns* (The 10 kingdoms of the coalition) *will hate the harlot. They will make her desolate and burn her with fire.* They will turn against Babylon.

Why do they turn against Babylon? Perhaps it's because she was so corrupt that she brought about nothing but chaos and destruction. Perhaps she was living in too much luxury at their expense. Perhaps they simply don't need her anymore because they have the "final solution" in sight; which is the total destruction of Israel at Armageddon.

We only know that **verse 17** tells us *God has put in the hearts of these 10 kings to fulfill **His will***.

But the effects of the seven bowls judgment will be the destruction of "Babylon" the headquarter city of this wicked world system; probably the result of a nuclear blast.

At this point in time, the antichrist's hope of a successful One World Empire of his own is gone, but his hope of destroying the 144,000 Jews at Armageddon is still alive.

REVELATION Chapter 18

The Fall of Babylon

Last 3 ½ years of the tribulation **The Wrath of God**

The last three verses of Chapter 17 imply that Babylon may have been destroyed by disgruntled allied forces *Rev.17:16-18*. It sounds as if the beast and the 10 kingdoms coalition has turned on Babylon *"and shall make her desolate, and naked, and shall eat her flesh, and to burn her with fire, for God has put in their heart to fulfill His will."*

God will use the 10 kingdom coalition, by which Babylon was supported, to destroy her; possibly with a relatively small nuclear bomb. It is the most probable way that a large metropolis could be destroyed and burned in one hour.

Rev.18: 1-4 *John sees a powerful angel come down from heaven, and the earth was lightened with his glory.* (Apparently, angels radiate light) *He cried with a mighty voice, saying," Babylon is fallen; Babylon is fallen, and is become the habitation of devils, and a cage for every foul spirit and hateful bird."* Babylon has become a rat infested pile of rubble.

After Babylon is lying in ruins, John hears a voice from heaven saying *"Come out of her **my people**; be not partakers of her sin and receive not her plagues."*

Apparently there were some decent people living there who missed the rapture of believers, but somehow survived the nuclear blast. Jesus might be knocking on the door of their heart, and calling them to come out of their sinful life style, and invite Him into their heart as Lord and Savior.

~~~~~~

Rev. 18: 5-7 *the sins of this great city Babylon have reached unto heaven and God has remembered every last one of them.*

Obadiah 1:15 says *"For the day of the Lord is near upon all the heathen: as you have done, it shall be done unto you: your reward shall return upon your own head."*

Verse 6 Rewarding Babylon double according to her works is **not** unjust punishment on God's part. She was not only drunk with the blood of the saints and martyrs, but due to her lack of remorse and her arrogant life style, God has doubled her reward.

Rev. 18: 8-12 Babylon's punishment will be quick. One day *when she thinks she is safe and secure, death, morning, famine, and fire will consume her.*

The kings of the earth who engaged in immorality with her are now lamenting her loss. From afar off they can see the devastating judgment of God that took place in one hour. Most likely they keep their distance to avoid radiation fallout from the nuclear blast. Obviously they had a strong emotional attachment to this metropolitan harlot.

Keep in mind that the harlot is not a literal woman. It will be a beautiful, but evil metropolitan city, and a corrupt world system that influences the morals of the entire world. It will probably be located somewhere in the former Roman Empire.

Rev. 18: 13-19 the merchants have no market for their merchandise such as gold, silver, precious stones, ivory, grain, cattle, fruits, **slaves, and the souls of men.** That these merchants trade in slavery, and human trafficking shows how truly evil and heartless these people are. *This great city will be made desolate in one hour.*

Rev. 18: 20 *the voice from heaven calls for rejoicing over the destruction of Babylon. The voice tells all who are in heaven including the holy apostles and prophets to celebrate because God has avenged them.*

Rev. 18: 21–24 *never again will Babylon deceive the nations.* Never again will she shed the blood of the martyrs, and live in luxury without remorse. Never again will she blaspheme the name of the Lord; *because in her was found the blood of the prophets, and saints, and all who were slain upon the earth throughout the ages.*

REVELATION Chapter 19 B

Battle of Armageddon

Last 3 ½ years of the tribulation **The Wrath of God**

In the first 10 verses of Ch.19 we were looking at the wedding feast of the Lamb and His bride. This most likely occurs at about mid-tribulation. But now in verses 11-21 we are looking at the battle of Armageddon which happens at the end of the 7 years of tribulation.

Rev.19: 11-13 *John sees heaven opened and a white horse whose rider is Jesus. The rider is called "Faithful and True and in righteousness He will judge and make war."*

The rider on the white horse is described as having *eyes as flames of fire, on his head were many crowns, his vesture dipped in blood, and His name is, The Word of God.* Jesus' vesture dipped in blood could be from treading the wine press of the wrath of God *Rev.14:18-20.* Those were the grapes of wrath spoken of in *Joel 3:13.*

Rev.19: 14 His white horse represents a conquering leader. *As He leads; the armies of heaven follow him on white horses wearing white linen* (Representing righteousness). One can almost hear them singing as they ride *"Victory in Jesus my Savior forever."*

This heavenly army, which is the bride of Christ, is about to leave heaven, and come to earth with Jesus as their conquering leader to fight at the battle of Armageddon.

I used to think, once in heaven always in heaven, but here we are leaving heaven in our resurrected bodies, and coming back to earth with our bridegroom to fight the battle of Armageddon. Rest assured we will never need to leave the New Heaven in *Rev.21:1.*

Rev. 21:1 *I saw a new heaven and a new earth: for the first heaven and the first earth were passed away; and there was no more sea.*

Rev. 19:15 *Out of His mouth goes a sharp sword which is the word of God. Heb.4:12 says the word of God is sharper than any two edged sword. With the word of God He will smite the nations.* He will defeat the coalition of 10 kings, and their multi-national forces with the words of His mouth.

Rev. 19:16 *King of Kings, Lord of Lords is written on the thigh of His vesture* as He rides the white horse making it visible for anyone to see.

Question: Is this the second return of Christ to the earth? **Yes,** but it has nothing to do with the rapture of believers when Jesus meets us in the air *I Thess.4:16-17*. At the rapture Jesus comes *for us*, but when He returns to earth to fight the battle of Armageddon; He will come **with us,** or should I say, **we** will come **with Him.**

Rev. 19:17-18 *John saw an angel stand high in the sky, announcing to all the vultures and scavengers to gather themselves to the supper of the great God. On the menu is the flesh of kings, captains, mighty men of the earth, and every level of society.* This is in reference to the battle of Armageddon.

Rev. 19:19 *John sees the beast (antichrist) and the kings, and their armies. They are gathered together to make war against Him that sat on the white horse, and against His army.*

Apparently, Gog and Magog (An anti-Semitic territory north of Israel, **not** directly associated with the 10 kingdom coalition) are also part of the attacking forces. This territory north of Israel is likely to be Russia.

Ezekiel 39:1-5 "KJV" (Paraphrased) *says, son of man prophesy against Gog. This says the Lord God; Behold, I am against you,* **O Gog, I will turn you back and leave but a sixth part of you.** *I will cause you to come up from the north parts, and bring you upon the mountains of Israel; you will fall on the mountains of Israel; you and the people who are with you. I will give your bodies to the ravenous birds and the scavengers of the field* (Referring to the battle of Armageddon). Remember: <u>**a sixth part** of Gog and their descendants will survive Armageddon to attack Israel again at the end of the millennium.</u>

Jesus is now coming as the Lion of Judah to fight the battle of Armageddon. His goal is to avenge His saints, overthrow the wicked world system (the 10 kingdom coalition), and establish His Kingdom of righteousness on earth (The 1000 year millennium).

His primary weapon is a sharp sword that comes from His mouth. With this sword He will smite the nations; meaning that whatever He says, will bring about their destruction.

It is quite possible that whatever Jesus says to them will be so wise and so clever that it will literally cause them to turn on each other, and fight each other to the death.

There are other examples of this happening in the Old Testament. When armies were about to fight against Israel; they end up fighting each other instead. For example, Judges 7: 16-23, and Ezekiel 38:18, 21.

Ezekiel 38: 18, 21 (paraphrased) says: *"When Gog shall come against the land of Israel, says the Lord God that my fury shall come up in my face. V.21 I will call for a sword against him throughout all my mountains, says the Lord God: every man's sword shall be against his brother."* So, they will fight each other to the death.

As His bride, we will be there at Armageddon, but because they will fight each other, we may **not** have to fight at all. Jesus has even made arrangements for the battle field to be cleaned up afterward by vultures and scavengers. *Rev.19: 17-18*

Even with the help of the vultures and scavengers, it will still take Israel seven months to bury the dead according to *Ezekiel 39: 11-12*

Ezekiel 39: 11-12 *It shall come to pass in that day, that I will give unto Gog a place there of graves in Israel, the valley of the passengers on the east of the sea: and I shall stop the noses of passengers: and there shall they bury Gog and all his multitude: and they shall call it the valley of Ha-mon-gog. And seven month shall the house of Israel be burying them, that they may cleanse the land.*

Two of the earliest casualties of this war will be the beast (antichrist), and the false prophet who performed miracles to deceive those who received the mark of the beast or worshipped his image. *Rev.13: 11-14*

Rev.19: 20 *Both of them (antichrist and false prophet) will be cast alive into the lake of fire that was **created for the devil and his angels** Matt.25: 41. The lake of fire was **not** originally created for people. It was created for the devil and his angels. Nevertheless, those who reject Jesus Christ, and identify themselves with the devil and his angels will go there.

Rev.20:10 says, *they shall be tormented day and night for ever and ever.* Can you imagine what that would be like? No relief, no rest, no mercy, no hope, nothing but pain, and regret for all eternity.

Rev.19: 21 *the remnant of the multi-national coalition who did* **not** *kill each other, were slain with the sword of Him that sat upon the white horse.* Jesus finished them off. It was they who conspired with the antichrist to shed the blood of the saints and martyrs; so we don't need to feel sorry for these people.

They refused a decent burial for the two witnesses in Ch.11, and gloated over their deaths. Now the fowls of the air will gorge themselves on the flesh of these arrogant fools.

After the battle of Armageddon there will still be many people on earth who have somehow survived the great tribulation, and the wrath of God. Although they missed the rapture, they did **not** willingly take the mark of the beast, nor did they participate in the battle at Armageddon. Many of them actively opposed the antichrist.

These tribulation survivors have **not** accepted Jesus Christ as their personal Savior. Nevertheless, by the Grace of God they still have a chance to be saved as Jesus begins to set up His kingdom on earth; the millennial reign of Christ.

REVELATION Chapter 20 A
Satan Arrested and Imprisoned 1000 years

The millennial reign of Christ

Rev.19: 20 said that during the battle at Armageddon the antichrist, and the false prophet were both cast alive into the lake of fire burning with brimstone; but what about Satan, the third member of the unholy trinity. Why he wasn't also cast into the lake of fire?

Remember, God has not yet proven that all of His promises to Israel will be fulfilled, so legally, Satan cannot be cast into the lake of fire, because legally, he still has the right to challenge God's truthfulness. However, he can be arrested and detained.

Rev.20: 1-2 John sees an angel (*officer*) descend from heaven (*the justice center*) with the key (*jailer's key*) to the bottomless pit (*jail*), and with a chain (*hand cuffs*) in his hand.

He laid hold of (*arrested*) the dragon, *also known as* the serpent, *also known as* the Devil, *also known as* Satan (*the criminal*), and bound him (*cuffed him)*, and cast him *(stuffed him*) into the bottomless pit (*the slammer*) for 1000 years. ***Yahoo!!!***

Rev.20: 3 this lawless, vicious, threat to society is bound. The King James Version says *he's "shut up" and sealed.* (Satan is shut up, and sealed shut for 1000 years). The reason he is locked up, and sealed is so he cannot deceive the nations for 1000 years.

After Satan's defeat in the war that occurred in heaven against Michael and his angels *(Ch.11)*, Satan lost free access to heaven, and was then cast down to earth. *Rev.12: 7-9* He lost a lot of his rank and authority.

He later loses his chief city of Babylon, and the battle at Armageddon. Then he is imprisoned for 1000 years, and looses his ability to move about, and to deceive the nations. Satan is continuously degraded, and ultimately defeated. Satan is a loser!

However, after the 1000 years are fulfilled, Satan must be released for a short time. We will learn more about why he is released later.

Jesus is about to set up His Kingdom on earth called the millennial reign of Christ. During that 1000 years Satan will be jailed in the bottomless pit. I don't know for sure if the bottomless pit is Hades, but if it is, then Satan will be locked up in his own jail.

Most believers accept that a "glorified Jesus" will return physically to earth at His second coming to fight, and win the battle of Armageddon. Then He will establish an earthly Kingdom where He will reign from the throne of David for 1000 years. Many of the Old Testament promises to Israel will be fulfilled at that time of peace.

Rev.20: 4 *John sees in heaven the thrones and they that sat upon them, and judgment was given unto them: and I saw the souls of them that were beheaded for the witness of Jesus, and for the word of God, and which had not worshiped the beast, neither his image, neither had received his mark upon their foreheads, or in their hands; and they lived and reigned with Christ a thousand years. V.5 But the rest of the dead lived not again until the thousand years were finished. This is the <u>first resurrection.</u> (For them)*

The first resurrection for <u>believers</u> was when *the Lord Himself shall descend from heaven with a shout, with the voice of the archangel, and with the trump of God: and the dead in Christ shall rise first: Then we which are alive and remain shall be caught up together with them* **in the air**: *and so shall we ever be with the Lord. I Thessalonians 4:16, 17.*

The first resurrection for <u>unbelievers</u> is in Rev. 20: 5 *But the rest of the dead (the lost) lived* **not** *until the 1000 years were finished. This is the <u>first resurrection</u>* (For them).

Lost people in graves will stay there another 1000 years before they are judged. The first resurrection (for believers) is before the 1000 years. The first, and only, resurrection (for unbelievers) is after the 1000 year Reign of Christ. It's called "The Great White Throne Judgment."

Rev. 20:6 says: *Blessed and holy is he that hath part in the first resurrection: on such the second death* (The lake of fire) *hath no power, but they* (of the first resurrection) *shall be priests of God and of Christ, and shall reign with Him a thousand years."*

~~~~~~

There are three huge people groups that will continue to exist on earth during the 1000 year reign of Christ.

1. The first group is Jesus and His glorified bride, which is the body of Christ. They will have resurrected bodies.
2. The second group is the faithful 144,000 Jewish believers in their natural human bodies. However, during the 1000 years they will die off, and go to be with the Lord. They will not procreate because they are described as virgins *Rev. 14:1-4*. They will receive their resurrected bodies at the Great White Throne judgment at the end of the millennium.
3. The third group is the unsaved tribulation survivors who **did not** willingly accept the mark of the beast. They will be in the millennium in their natural human bodies. *Isaiah 2:4* says something interesting about the tribulation survivors who missed the rapture, but **did not** take the mark of the beast.

When Jesus sits on His millennial throne, and separates the sheep from the goats: *He shall judge among the nations, and shall rebuke many people: and they shall beat their swords into plowshares, and their spears into pruning hooks: nation shall not lift up sword against nation; neither shall they learn war any more.*

Jesus neither praises nor condemns them, but He rebukes them (He informs and instructs them), and they listen. Who are these former warriors? They are **unsaved** tribulation survivors who did not take the mark of the beast. Many of them actively opposed the antichrist during the tribulation, and when Jesus rebukes them they will give up their weapons, and live in peace with their fellow man.

These are decent people who missed the rapture, but still opposed the antichrist, and somehow survived the great tribulation. Unfortunately, a lot of decent people will miss the rapture. These could be honorable people who believe in truth and justice. People who sit in church every Sunday, hungry and thirsty for spiritual truth, but never hear the gospel of Jesus Christ preached correctly. It may have been more the fault of their spiritual leaders than of themselves.

These are people who could have been saved if someone would have bothered to witness to them. Perhaps this is when *Jesus will sit upon His millennial throne, and gather before Him all the nations of the world to separate the sheep from the goats. Matt. 25: 31-46*

The sheep on His right hand could be those who opposed the antichrist, and aided the people of God, be they Jews or Christians, during the first 3 ½ years of the tribulation even though they didn't know they were serving Jesus. Although they were **not** part of the rapture harvest, they were **spared,** and will possibly be **gleaned** for the Lord during the millennial reign of Christ.

The goats on His left hand could be those tribulation survivors who **did** willingly receive the mark of the beast. They will be eliminated by the angels. *Matt.13: 41- 42*

Matt.13: 41-42 *the Son of man shall send forth His angels, and they shall gather out of His kingdom all things that offend, and them which do iniquity; and shall cast them into a furnace of fire: there shall be wailing and gnashing of teeth.*

Some people say only believers will go into the millennium, but if that were true, why would Jesus need to rule with a rod of iron *Rev.19:15*, and why would it be necessary for Satan to be released for a short time after the 1000 years. Who are the people Satan will rally to a huge final battle against the holy city, and the saints of God? *Rev.20:7-9*

REVELATION Chapter 20 B
Jesus Separates the Sheep from the Goats

Matt.25: 31 *When the Son of man shall come in His glory and the holy angels with Him; then shall He sit upon the throne of His glory.*

When does this happen? It probably happens right after Jesus returns to earth to fight, and win the battle of Armageddon. Then He will begin to reign on earth for 1000 years as He sits on the throne of His glory.

Matt.25: 32 *and before Him shall be gathered all nations: and He shall separate them one from another, as a shepherd divides his sheep from his goats.*

This judgment has nothing to do with a resurrection from the dead. The angels will gather all nations to King Jesus for the purpose of sorting, and separating tribulation survivors as to who will be allowed to enter into the earthly Kingdom of Jesus Christ, and who will be eliminated, and sent to Hades. What criteria will Jesus use for this judgment?

Matt.25: 33-36 *He shall sit the sheep on His right hand, but the goats on His left. Then shall the King say unto the sheep on His right hand. Come ye blessed of my Father, inherit the kingdom prepared for you from the foundation of the world. For I was an hungered, and ye gave me meat: I was thirsty, and ye gave me drink: I was a stranger, and ye took me in: naked and ye clothed me: I was sick, and ye visited me: I was in prison, and ye came unto me.*

Notice: all of these commendations for inheriting the earthly kingdom are based on their good deeds; not necessarily their faith in Jesus. These are tribulation survivors who were **not** saved, but did oppose the antichrist by not taking the mark; and did do right by their fellow man.

Matt.25: 37-39 Then shall the righteous answer (paraphrased) *Lord, when did we do all those things for you?* Why couldn't they remember doing good things for the Lord?

They knew they did those things, but they didn't know they were serving the Lord. ***Opposing evil is serving the Lord.*** Jesus said: *You're either with me or against me.* So there will be unsaved people during the tribulation who will risk their lives to oppose the evil of the antichrist without knowing they are doing God a service.

They are called righteous because they did the **right** thing by opposing the antichrist, and helping God's people even though their help was **not** based on faith, but a common sense of truth, justice, and common decency. They were **not** saved to enter heaven, but to continue their lives on this earth. They could be predestinated from the foundation of the world to be saved during the millennial reign of Christ.

Their works of wood, hay, and stubble may be burned up, and have no eternal value because they were not done in the name of Jesus. *Yet they themselves might be saved, so as by fire. I Corin.3: 11-15*

Matt.25: 40 *and the King shall answer and say unto them, Verily I say unto you, insomuch as ye have done it unto one of the least of these my brothers, ye have done it unto me.* They were **not saved** by their good works, but they were **spared** because their good works identified whose side they were on; the side of righteousness, the side of God's people. God promised to bless those who bless His people. *Gen.12: 3*

Remember Joshua chapter 2: when Joshua sent the two spies to Jericho, where they were hidden and protected by Rahab, the pagan prostitute, because she had heard that their God had miraculously delivered the Israelites from the bondage of Egypt. She was not part of the people of God, and yet she and her family were **spared** from destruction at Jericho, and later included into the family of God.

Hebrews 11:31 *by faith the harlot Rahab perished **not** with them that believed **not**, when she had received the spies with peace.* She showed favor to God's people.

Rahab was not saved by her good works, but she was **spared** from condemnation because of her fear and reverence of the only true God. She rejected pagan worship, and aided the people of God. Her good works identified whose side she was on; the side of righteousness.

After the tribulation of her time was over she was formally included into the family of God by faith.

During WWII some Germans opposed Hitler, and aided the Jews. They were on the side of righteousness. After the war they were recognized as heroes. *Example: Oscar Schindler*

Matt.25: 41-43 *then shall He say unto them on the left hand. Depart from me you cursed, into everlasting fire, prepared for the devil and his angels: for I was an hungered and ye gave me no meat; I was thirsty, and ye gave me no drink: I was a stranger and ye took me not in: naked and ye clothed me not: sick, and in prison and ye visited me not.*

Matt.25: 44 Then shall they also answer Him saying (paraphrased) *Lord, when did we **not** minister to your needs?*

Matt.25: 45 *Then shall He answer them, saying, verily, I say unto you, insomuch as ye did it **not** unto one of the least of these, ye did it **not** unto me.* They obviously had an opportunity to help God's people during their time of affliction, but they didn't do it. So, whether they took the mark or not, they identified themselves with the devil and his angels. They were merciless to God's people.

Matt.25: 46 Jesus said *"These shall go away into everlasting punishment: but the righteous into life eternal."* Most likely the angels will execute those on the left. They will die in their sins, and go to Hades.

As for those who missed the rapture due to unbelief; few if any will be "born again" during the wrath of God. However, some tribulation survivors will have another chance to be saved during the millennial reign of Christ. They may be counted as sheep, and allowed to live in the earthly Kingdom of Jesus Christ where they will hopefully be led to a personal relationship with Jesus. God is not willing that any should perish. What a gracious Savior He is!

REVELATION Chapter 20 C

What is the purpose of the 1000 year millennium?

When Christ Jesus reigns on earth with a scepter of righteousness it will be a time of love, peace, and safety for all who inhabit the earth, because Satan is bound.

Isaiah 11: 6-9 (Paraphrased) *The wolf shall dwell with the lamb, and the leopard shall lie down with the kid; and the calf and the young lion together; and a little child shall lead them. The cow and the bear shall feed; their young ones shall lie down together: and the lion shall eat straw like the ox. The sucking child shall play on the hole of the Asp. They shall not hurt or destroy in all my holy mountain: the earth shall be full of the knowledge of the Lord, as the waters cover the sea.*

Notice that the lion will eat straw like the ox. The lion will no longer be carnivorous. Wild animals will be tame. The knowledge and spirit of the Lord will be prevalent throughout the world. All eyes and ears will be focused of King Jesus who will rule from the throne of David in Jerusalem.

The Saints of God will be assigned millennial areas of authority. They will rule, and represent King Jesus in specific locations throughout the world. Our inheritances, and rewards, are based on our present earthly faithfulness, service, and perseverance for Christ. (Example)

Luke 19: 12-19 (paraphrased) Jesus said: *A certain nobleman went into a far country to receive for himself a kingdom and to return. And he called his ten servants, and delivered them ten pounds, and said unto them, occupy till I come. But his citizens hated him, and sent a message after him, saying: We will not have this man to reign over us. And it came to pass, that when he was returned, when he had received the kingdom, then he commanded* *these servants to be called unto him, that he might know how much every man had gained by trading.*

V.16, 17 *Then came the first, saying, Lord, thy pound hath gained ten pounds. And he said unto him, well, thou good servant: because thou hast been faithful in a very little, have thou authority over ten cities.* (Ten cities in the millennium is a lot of people)

V.18, 19 *And the second came, saying, Lord thy pound hath gained five pounds. And he said likewise to him, be thou also over five cities.*

Rev. 5: 9-10 the **redeemed** of the Lord will be kings and priests who will rule and reign on earth with Christ for 1000 years; **but over whom will they rule and reign?**

Who will live in these cities? There will be many people who have somehow made it through the great tribulation without choosing to take the mark of the beast. They were **not** involved in the battle of Armageddon, **nor** have they received Jesus Christ in their lifetime. These are people who still have a chance to be saved during the millennium.

Satan is bound, so he is **not** present to deceive them. If they show any sign of rebellion against the King, immediate punitive action will be taken against them. They will be killed as Christ will rule, not only with a scepter of righteousness, but also with a rod of iron. Rev.19:15

The purpose of the millennium might be for God to prove that man's heart is evil by his Adamic nature. Because we are all descendants of Adam; man has a propensity to sin with or without the influence of Satan. They cannot say "The devil made me do it."

Another purpose of the millennium is that many of the promises to Israel will be accomplished at that time of enduring peace, which could only happen in the millennium when Jesus reigns, and Satan is bound.

Another purpose of the millennium is to glean the four corners of the earth after the main harvest of believers (The rapture). Many tribulation survivors will be saved during this 1000 year time of peace, when Satan is bound. There will probably be a population explosion on the earth. These unsaved tribulation survivors who are still on earth need to be indoctrinated into the Christian faith; but by whom?

Rev.20: 6 the redeemed priests of God are to indoctrinate these people into the Christian faith during the 1000 year reign of Christ. The redeemed priests of God are us. We will attempt to lead these tribulation survivors (The sheep) to King Jesus. This might be the gleaning of the four corners of the earth after the main harvest known as the first resurrection (or rapture) has been accomplished.

Most people who say the prayer that Jesus taught in Matt.6: 9-13 don't realize that when they say *"Thy kingdom come, thy will be done, on earth as it is in heaven"*, could actually be referring to "the millennial reign of Christ", as well as this present age of grace.

During the 1000 year millennial reign of Christ on earth, there are three major groups that will be there. The **first group:** Jesus and His bride (the body of Christ) will reign with immortal resurrected bodies as priests of God.

The **Second group:** The 144,000 faithful Jewish believers will have mortal bodies, and will die off during the 1000 year millennium because *Rev.14: 1-4* describes them as virgins. They will be resurrected at the great white throne judgment.

The **third group** is the tribulation survivors who **did not** take the mark of the beast. They will be there in mortal bodies, and they will reproduce. The tribulation survivors were the sheep who were on His right hand, while the goats on His left hand were eliminated.

How these mortal beings will interact with the immortal beings is a mystery, but it will probably be like it was when Jesus, in his resurrected body, interacted with the two disciples on the road to Emmaus, *Luke 24:13-43*, or with His disciples in the upper room after His resurrection. *John 20: 26-29*

During that 1000 years Satan will be bound, and there will be a population explosion on this earth. People who die during those 1000 years will either go to heaven or hell just as they do now. They will be resurrected, and judged at the great white throne judgment at the end of the millennium. *John 5: 28-29*

John 5: 28-29 *Marvel not at this: for the hour is coming, in the which all that are in the graves shall hear his voice, and shall come forth; they that have done good, unto the resurrection of life; and they that have done evil, unto the resurrection of damnation.*

Notice that the great white throne, unlike the first resurrection (the rapture of believers), is the only judgment in which both the good, and the evil are resurrected at the same time. The good are tribulation survivors saved during the millennial reign of Christ.

The evil are all those of every generation who's names are **not** written in the Lamb's book of life due to unbelief. We will learn more about the great white throne judgment later.

Foot Note:

By the way: the two disciples on the road to Emmaus in *Luke 24:13-43* were not likely to be two men as many people assume, but rather a man and his wife. The man's name was Cleophas, and we know he was married because one of the Marys' at the foot of the cross was Mary the wife of Cleophas. *John 19:25*.

When they reached Emmaus Jesus would have gone on, but they both constrained Him to abide with them and eat. The fact that Cleophas was married, and they "both" invited Jesus in for supper is at least some evidence that they were a man and his wife, while there is no evidence that they were two men.

REVELATION Chapter 20 D
Satan Released a for Short Time

Rev.20: 7 *after the thousand years are completed; Satan must be released from his prison* (the bottomless pit). He will return to his same activities as before to deceive the nations in the four quarters of the earth (the entire world).

So far Satan has succeeded in deceiving the Jewish people for over 2000 years, as they still do **not** accept Jesus as their Messiah. During the great tribulation they will awaken from their spiritual slumber that they are in for crucifying Jesus, and they will know that Jesus is their true Messiah. When Satan can no longer deceive the Jewish people, he will try to destroy them.

At the beginning of the 7 years of tribulation the antichrist made a peace treaty with the Jews. When Israel is finished building their temple in Jerusalem, after 3 ½ years the antichrist will break the treaty, and try to destroy them.

God protected, and nurtured them the last 3 ½ years of the great tribulation. Then the antichrist tried to drive them into the Mediterranean Sea at Armageddon, and failed. Now after 1000 years of peace, Satan is released, and has one last chance to destroy Israel.

Rev.20: 8 *Satan is released, and again he goes out to deceive the nations of the world.* He will point out to the nations the difference between what they have **compared** to what Israel, and Jerusalem have. Jerusalem will be the capital city of the world during the millennial reign of Christ.

The earthly Kingdom and Throne of Jesus Christ will be lavish, and glorious; well beyond that of Solomon's kingdom temple. *Isaiah 11: 9 tells us the earth shall be filled with the knowledge of the Lord at that time.*

Can you imagine that? No doubt the world will lavish gifts on the King just as the wise men did when the King was born in Bethlehem.

Psalms 68: 29 says: *Because of your temple at Jerusalem kings will bring you gifts.*

I Kings 10:10 the Queen of Sheba brought gifts to King Solomon, etc.

When Satan is released he will introduce to the world a concept that had never really crossed their minds while he was bound. Satan will instill **envy** and **jealousy** into the nations, and tempt them to "**spread the wealth**", and to level the playing field, so to speak.

Up till this time the faith and commitment of the tribulation survivors, and their descendants had **not** been tested. They were easily led to the Lord while Satan was bound, but when tested many of them will fall for Satan's deception, and prove that their commitment was not real. They will agree to help plunder Israel. Tribulation survivors are the only possible source of these rebellious warriors.

Satan will gather innumerable multi-national forces including Gog and Magog (an anti Semitic territory north of Israel **not** directly associated with the 10 kingdom coalition.) This territory north of Israel is probably Russia. These forces combine to surround, destroy, and plunder Israel. The original 10 kingdom coalition of the antichrist will **not** be involved in this battle because they were destroyed at the battle of Armageddon.

However...**Ezekiel 39:1-2** "KJV" *tells us that* **a sixth part** *of Gog and Magog were spared at the battle of Armageddon prior to the 1000 year millennial reign of Christ. That* **sixth part**, *or rather their descendants, will live to fight again in this final battle.*

Ezekiel Chapter 38 is addressing this future battle that will occur at the end of the 1000 year millennium when Satan is released, and goes out to rally the nations to plunder Israel. The people involved will be the greatly multiplied descendants of that 1/6 part of Gog (Russia) that survived the battle of Armageddon.

Ezekiel Ch.38: 3-4 (paraphrased) *I am against thee, Oh Gog, the chief prince of Meshech and Tubal. (Russia) I will turn you back, and put hooks into your jaws, and bring you forth and all your army.*

***V.8** In the latter years* you shall come into the land that is brought back, and is gathered out of many people, (Israel was brought back as a nation in 1948) **they that dwell safely.** (In the millennium)

Ezekiel 38: 9-19 *you will come like a storm, like a cloud to cover the land, you and all your bands.*

V.10 *At that time shall things come into your mind, and you shall think an evil thought.*

V.11 you will say, *"I will go up to the land of the un-walled villages. I will go to them that are at rest that dwell safely without walls, bars, or gates."*

V.12-13 *to take a spoil and a pray; and turn thy hand upon the people that are gathered out of the nations that have gotten cattle and goods and silver and gold.*

V.14-16 *Therefore, Ezekiel prophecy and say unto Gog,* "*when my people Israel dwell safely, and you shall come out of the north against my people Israel as a cloud that covers the land it shall be in the latter days."* (After the millennium)

V.18-19 *my fury shall come up in my face, and in my jealousy, and in the fire of my wrath there shall be a great shaking in the land of Israel. V.22 and I will rain upon him, and his bands great hailstones, fire, and brimstone.* There is a parallel verse in *Rev.20: 9.*

Rev.20: 9 *when they surround the beloved City of God* (Jerusalem), *fire will come down out of heaven, and devour them.*

Rev.20: 10 *at that time the devil is cast into the lake of fire where the beast and the false prophet are, and shall be tormented day and night forever and ever.* At that time Satan's worst fear will become his reality.

The un-holy trinity will not cease to exist. Their annihilation would be an act of mercy, but they will receive no mercy. There is no need of a formal trial for the unholy trinity. They were in direct opposition to God on every front. *Genesis to Revelation is Satan's trial time.*

REVELATION Chapter 20 E
The Great White Throne Judgment

The final judgment

Rev.20: 11 *John sees a **great white throne**, and Him that sat on the throne.* The one seated on the throne is Jesus, because *John 5:22* tells us: *the Father has entrusted all judgment to the Son.*

John sees something spectacular: *the earth and heaven fled from the presence of Him that sat on the throne.* This could mean that Sovereign God will destroy the universe that He created including the earth itself which He calls *"the first heaven and the first earth." Rev.21: 1*

Rev.20: 12 *John sees the resurrected dead stand before the throne of God, and the books (plural) were opened. The Book of Life was also opened. The dead (lost) were judged out of those books according to their works.* (This is the second and final resurrection).

Q. Why books (plural)? A. There is probably one for every person who has ever lived; a detailed diary of their life.

The first earth will pass away, but verse 13 indicates that God will remove all the deceased for judgment before that happens. **V.13** *And the sea gave up the dead which were in it; and death and hell delivered up the dead which were in them: and they were judged every man according to their works.*

Rev.20: 5 these are *"the rest of the dead"* those who missed the first resurrection because of unbelief. They are judged out of the books (plural) containing their works. *Eph.2: 8-9 says they cannot be saved by their good works.* These books will contain every sin, every careless word, every secret thought, or deed they have ever committed.

The great white throne judgment is for people who **did not** have part in the first resurrection. This second resurrection is primarily for all the lost of every generation. However, there is another book that will be opened at the great white throne judgment. It is *"The Book of Life."*

By the grace of God, many who survived the great tribulation, and their descendants, will be saved during the 1000 year reign of Christ. These people are primarily Gentiles who survived the great tribulation without taking the mark of the beast. Many of them will be led to the Lord by the saints who reign as priests of God in the millennium. *Rev.20: 6*

Rev.20: 6 *"Blessed and holy is he that has part in the first resurrection: on such the second death has no power* (no condemnation) *but they shall be priests of God and of Christ, and shall reign with Him for one thousand years."* These priests will lead many of the tribulation survivors to King Jesus. They will glean the four corners of the earth.

Those who are led to the Lord during the millennium will be resurrected to life at the great white throne judgment. Their names will be in the Lambs Book of Life, and they will be welcomed into the New Heaven.

Rev.20: 13-15 tells us *"death and hell"* were cast into the lake of fire, **and whosever's name was not written in the book of life was cast into the lake of fire** *which is the second death*. That could be anyone who rejects Jesus Christ as their personal Savior.

The first death is physical death. The second death is complete separation from God.

Hell was a temporary holding place for the lost, but at the white throne judgment un-believers will be transferred from jail to prison *(The lake of fire)* for eternity.

We need to be absolutely certain that our name is written in the *Lamb's Book of Life*. John 3: 3 says: Except a man be "born again", he cannot see the kingdom of God. So it's very important that we know……
How to be a Born Again Christian.

How to be a Born Again Christian

1. **Confession:** Agree with God that you are a sinner. We are sinners, not because we sin, but because we have a sinful nature. We did not become sinners by sinning. We were born with the propensity to sin, because of our selfish nature.

2. **Repentance:** Being sincerely sorry for every sin you have ever committed. We should love what God loves, and hate what God hates. We should hate sin because God hates sin, but He **does not** hate sinners.

3. **Believe:** that Jesus Christ is the sinless Son of God, and that the innocent blood He shed on the cross was sufficient for the forgiveness of your sins. Faith is taking God at His word (the bible).

4. **Invite** Jesus Christ to come into your heart, and be the Lord of your life. Jesus said "I stand at the door (of your heart), and knock. If any man invites me in I will come in." *Rev.3:20*

    Whosoever shall call on the name of the Lord shall be saved. *Acts 2:21*

5. **Ask** God to fill you with the Holy Spirit, and help you understand His word (the bible), and His will for your life. Teaching and understanding **is** a function of the Holy Spirit, the third person of the trinity.

6. **Thank, Praise, and Serve** God for giving you the gift of eternal life. Then we must grow into spiritual maturity. This takes time, experience, and a grateful heart. Remember that your second birth is just as real, and just as important as your first birth.

REVELATION Chapter 20F
G.W.T. Chart

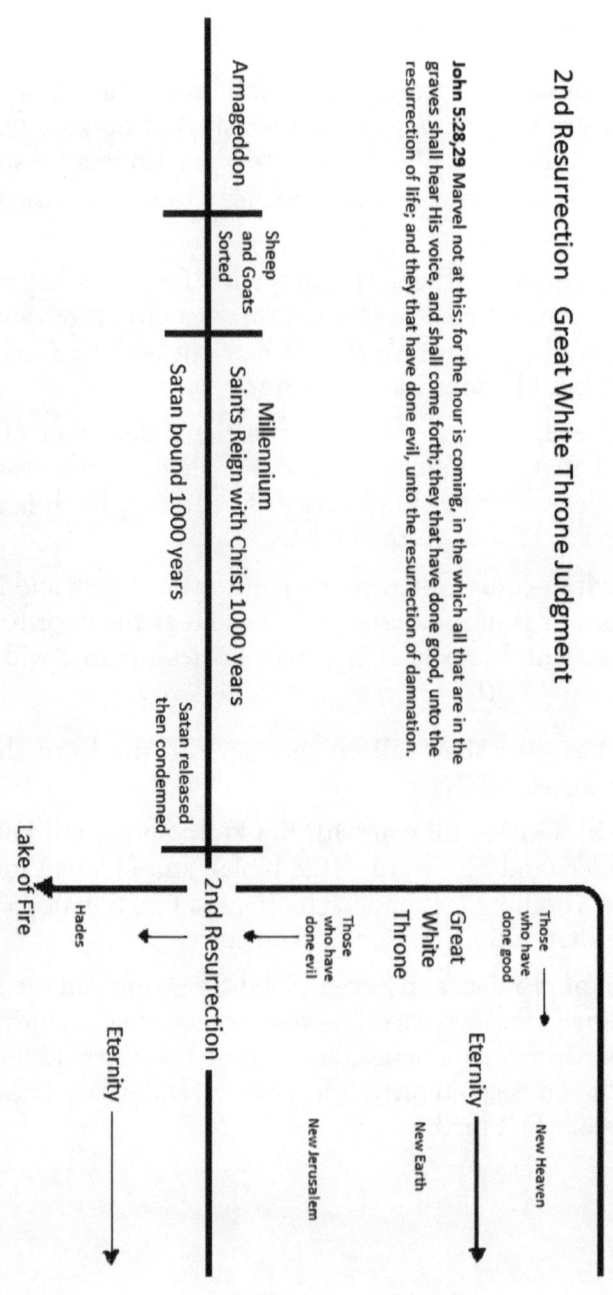

REVELATION Chapter 21
The New Heaven, New Earth, and New Jerusalem

Rev.21: 1 *John sees a New Heaven, and a New Earth, for the first heaven and earth had passed away.* The question is: Why did they pass away, and how did they pass away?

Why this present earth must pass away is answered best in **Rom. 8: 21-22:** *The creature itself also shall be delivered from the bondage of corruption into the glorious liberty of the children of God. For we know that the whole creation groaneth and travaileth in pain together until now.*

This sin laden world needs to be delivered from the bondage of corruption, as it groans and travails in suffering and degradation. Some think this earth will be restored, and continue on forever, but Rev.21:5 says, "**God will make all things new.**" This old earth will **not** be renewed. "Renewal" is impossible because "New" can only happen once.

II Corin.4: 4 tell us that *"the god of this world has blinded the minds of them which believe not."* Would the saints of God want to live in a remodeled world that was once grossly dysfunctional due to the pride, cruelty, and deception of the devil? God wouldn't want that either. *Almighty God will make all things new. Rev.21:5*

II Peter 3: 10-12 tells us *"the heavens shall pass away with a great noise and the elements shall melt with fervent heat. The earth also, and the works that are therein shall be burned up."* Even rocks will melt, and every seed of new life will be burned up.

The New Earth will be completely different from this present earth. This earth is dysfunctional, and hopelessly out of order. It can't be fixed by man, and it won't be fixed by God. But the real issue on judgment day is the heart of each individual.

Psalms 34: 16 *the face of the Lord is against those who do evil, to cut off the memory of them from the earth.*

This might be a good thing because **if** we did remember lost people we might have a lot of sadness, and regrets to deal with in heaven. Loved ones who were spiritually lost and bound for hell may never be remembered, while faithful brothers and sisters will never be forgotten. There will be no sorrow in the New Heaven.

By the end of Chapter 20 of Revelation we see all those who would do evil, both human and angelic, have been cast into the lake of fire. Evil is gone forever.

Isaiah 65: 17-18 (paraphrased) tells us to *rejoice in the* **creation** *of a New Heaven, a New Earth, and a New Jerusalem, inhabited only by those who share the joy of knowing their Lord and Savior.*

Rev.21: 2 *John sees the New Jerusalem coming down from God out of heaven, prepared as a bride adorned for her husband* (It will be breathtakingly beautiful). Where does the New Jerusalem land? It lands on the New Earth.

Rev.21: 3 at that time God's most important unfulfilled prophecy to His chosen people will be fulfilled. Ezekiel 37: 27-28: *My tabernacle also shall be with them: yea, I will be their God, and they shall be my people. And the heathen shall know that I the Lord do sanctify Israel, when my sanctuary shall be in the midst of them for evermore.*

Rev.21: 4 we may not know much about what will be in the New Jerusalem, but we can know what will **not** be there. *No more tears, death, sorrow, pain, sickness, crying, headaches, heartaches,* or any such thing.

Rev.21: 5-6 Then He said to John *"Write: for these words are true and faithful. **It is** done." **What is done?*** God's justice has been served, and His people have been avenged. Evil in every form has been crushed and punished.

Now it is time for rewards. *Jesus is the author and finisher of our faith,* but our faith is not finished until His faithful saints have been glorified, and rewarded. The Lord says *"I will give unto him that is athirst of the fountain of the water of life freely."*

Rev.21: 7 God declares *"He that overcomes shall inherit **all** things; I will be his God, and he shall be my son."* The children of God are *joint heirs with Jesus Rom.8:17.* Jesus is God's only begotten son, and we are adopted children, but we are legally joint heirs with Jesus; **a truly mind boggling concept!**

Rev.21: 9-11 One of the 7 powerful angels who poured out the bowls says to John *"Come and I will show you the bride, the Lamb's wife."* He *carried John away in the spirit to a great high mountain, and showed him a great city, the Holy Jerusalem. The source of the splendor and brilliance of this city is the glory of God.*

John 14:3 *Jesus said "I go to prepare a place for you,* (My promised bride) *I will come again, and receive you unto myself; that where I am, there you may be also."*

This implies that our eternal home is being prepared every day as Jesus observes our every thought, word, and deed. It is uniquely designed for His eternal "soul mate." It perfectly reflects every need, desire, and passion His bride will ever experience. The New Jerusalem, as shown to John by the angel, literally *"represents"* the bride of Christ.

Rev. 21:12-13 *The city is surrounded by a wall on each of the four sides. On each wall there were 3 gates and on those 12 gates are the names of the 12 tribes of the children of Israel.* There is an angel stationed at each of the 12 gates. They are like greeters or tour guides. Unlike the cherubim who guarded against access to the tree of life after the fall of Adam and Eve in the Garden of Eden *Gen.3:24;* we will have full access to the tree of life.

Rev. 21:14 *"The wall of the city had **twelve foundations**, and in them the names of the twelve apostles of the Lamb."* Forevermore, the 12 gates will honor the 12 tribes of Old Testament Israel, and the 12 foundations will forever honor the New Testament apostles of the church of Christ. Together they honor the 24 elders.

"NEW JERUSALEM" The City that is Built Four Square

Rev. 21: 15-16 *the angel had a golden reed to measure the holy city, the gates, and the walls. The New Jerusalem measured four square: the length, breadth, and height of it being equal.* It measured twelve thousand furlongs, which would be at least 1400 miles in each direction, and then at least 1400 miles high.

The length, breadth, and height of the New Jerusalem are equal. What geometric figure does that remind you of? There are three geometric figures that can have the same length, breadth, and height. What are they?

They are a sphere, a cube, and a four sided pyramid. The question is: How can we know which one applies to the New Jerusalem in this case? Most commentators think the New Jerusalem will be shaped like a cube, but I don't think so.

The answer could be in verse 16; *the city lays "four square."* What does it mean for a geometric figure to lay four square? This means that, as a geometric figure it can only be squared (with a right angle carpenters square) in four different ways; no more, no less.

The sphere is eliminated because it cannot be squared at all. A cube is also eliminated because it lays 12 square. A cube can be squared 12 different ways. (Illustrate)

But a four sided **pyramid** can only be squared in four different ways. It can only be squared on each of the four corners at the base of the pyramid.

The four sided pyramid is therefore the only true four square geometric figure that exists. If the New Jerusalem is shaped like a four sided pyramid, it is truly ***"The City that is Built Four Square."*** The pyramid is also the most stable geometric figure in that it is the most difficult to topple. **Rev. 21:10** says *"the Holy City is shaped like a mountain."* Of the three geometric figures, the four sided pyramid is the only one shaped like a mountain.

An example of a four sided pyramid can be seen on the back of a one dollar bill, and the great pyramids of Egypt are also four sided pyramids.

Rev. 21: 17-20 without getting into the details, it suffices to say that this city is magnificent beyond our wildest imagination. The wall around the city is **not** to keep evil out, because there is no more evil, but rather to define the city's borders.

Rev. 21: 21 *the 12 gates were made of one pearl each, and the streets were made of purest gold as it were transparent glass.* Both defy human understanding, but what's really important is **not** what we see in the New Jerusalem, but who we see there. We will see Jesus face to face.

Rev. 21: 22 *there is no temple in the New Jerusalem.* Why is there no temple in the New Jerusalem? In the Old Testament the temple was a place of divine provision for sinful man. Through blood sacrifices and offerings, sinful man could come into the presence of God. There was a veil separating them, and only the high priest could enter once a year. *Heb. 9: 6-7*

Heb. 9:11-12 (paraphrased) but *Jesus, the Lamb of God and our high priest, entered the holy place, for our redemption, and offered* **not** *the blood of goats and calves, but His body, and His blood* **once for all**. In John 2:19-21 Jesus spoke of His body as being the temple of sacrifice. Therefore, since there will be no sin in heaven, a temple of sacrifice will no longer be necessary. Jesus sacrificed the temple of His body on earth.

Rev. 21: 23 *the city had no need of the sun or moon, for the glory of God, and of the Lamb did lighten it.* There is a parallel passage in *Isaiah 60:19*.

Isaiah 60: 19 *the sun shall be no more thy light by day; neither for brightness shall the moon give light unto thee: but the Lord shall be unto thee an everlasting light, and thy God, thy glory.* The New Earth will have no sun, moon, oceans, or seas. *Rev.21: 1*

John 8:12 *Jesus is the light of the world.* **That light** *came into the world, and men loved darkness rather than light because their sins were evil. John 3:19*

Rev. 21: 25-27 *the gates of the eternal city will never be shut. There is no night there* and no need of physical security. There will be no evil or corruption of any kind entering this city because only righteous people whose names are written in the Lambs Book of Life will live there. *They were once darkened by sin, but now they walk in the light of the Lord. Eph. 5: 8*

Since people die at different ages on earth, but live forever in heaven, you might wonder what age we are likely to be in heaven. Did you ever wonder about that? Whatever age it is it will probably never change. There will be no aging process there.

Mark 16:1-6 verses 5 and 6 say: "*entering into the sepulcher* (Tomb) *they saw* **a young man** *sitting on the right side clothed in white garment: and they were affrighted.*" *He saith unto them* "*be not affrighted: you seek Jesus of Nazareth which was crucified: He is risen: He is not here.*"

Most likely ***the young man*** at the tomb was an angel (In his prime). Luke 20:36 says, *"neither can they die anymore for they are equal to the angels: and are the children of God: being the children of the resurrection."* This could imply that our new glorified bodies ***might forever be young adults in our prime*** like the angels. Nevertheless, there will always be a difference between the angels, and the saints of God who have been redeemed, because angels cannot be redeemed once they have fallen.

REVELATION Chapter 22
The River and Tree of Life

Rev.22: 1-2 *The angel shows John a pure river of water of life, clear as crystal, flowing out of the throne of God and of the Lamb.*

Present day believers think of the Holy Spirit of God as a river of life flowing out from the throne of God. Jesus was speaking of the Holy Spirit when He offered living water to the woman at the well *John 4:10-14.* This is a visible river of life flowing from the throne that John can actually see.

On either side of the bank of the river, and in the midst of it, was the tree of life which yielded 12 manners of fruit, perhaps a different fruit for each month of the year. This might imply that there are months and years in heaven. If there is time in heaven it will be endless time.

This life giving water flows from the throne of God; it goes wherever God chooses as it flows out to the various nations on the New Earth. Yes, there will be nations, and a system of government on the New Earth. It will be a perfect theocratic government; not for the purpose of enforcing laws to protect anyone, but for the purpose of coordinating the beauty of order, and of symmetry. *Isaiah 9: 7*

Rev.21: *verse one* implies "there are no oceans, or seas on the New Earth," but there will be **no** shortage of waterways bringing living water to all of the inhabitants of the New Earth. If this present earth will be restored, and continue on forever, as some people say, where would the massive oceans and seas of this world go?

With no oceans or seas, much more of the New Earth will be inhabitable. There will be plenty of room for everyone including the billions of people who died prematurely as babies. It is likely that there will be rivers, streams, and maybe ponds and lakes, but no bodies of water large enough to constitute a sea or an ocean. *Rev.21: 1*

Isaiah 9: 7 says, **of the increase of His government and peace there shall be no end**, *upon the throne of David, and upon His Kingdom, to order it, and to establish it with judgment and with justice* **from henceforth even forever.** *The zeal of the Lord of hosts will perform this.*

This seems to say that whatever His eternal Kingdom is; unlike His 1000 year earthly Kingdom, there will be no end to the increase of it. The heavenly Kingdom of Jesus Christ will forever continue to *increase* and *expand*. In heaven no one will ever ask "Is this all there is, or have I seen it all?"

Did you ever open a computer website that had a lot of windows attached to it? Each time you opened a window there would be more links to click on. And when you click on them they open even more links. It seemed to expand endlessly, and interesting as it is, you soon realize that you don't have time for all of this. In heaven you will have all the time you need to investigate everything that interests you.

John 14: 3 Jesus said *"I go to prepare a place for you* (My bride), *I will come again, and receive you unto myself; that where I am, there ye may be also.* As the bride of Jesus we will be His helpmate. We will be intimately involved in everything that happens in the New Heaven. Our common goal will be to increase the glory, honor, comfort, and enjoyment of His Kingdom; which is our eternal home. We'll do it for Him, and for one another.

There will **not** be a monetary system on the New Earth, but Jesus did say that we should *store up for our selves treasures in heaven where moth and rust do not destroy, and where thieves do not break in and steal Matt.6:20.* It's true that we can't take anything with us when we die, but we can send treasures on to heaven before we get there.

Many of the treasures in heaven will be there because of the thoughtful prayers, precious words of wisdom, and sacrificial deeds of kindness that were done on this earth in secret. *The Father who sees what is done in secret will openly reward His faithful saints.*

Rev.22: 2 *the leaves of the tree are "for the healing of the nations."* The leaves of the tree of life seem to symbolize **perpetual healing** that God has provided for His saints on the New Earth.

Since there is no sickness on the New Earth, the leaves might be "preventative medicine". Perhaps it's **not** that we couldn't get sick or hurt, but that by God's design and protection, sicknesses, and debilitating accidents simply will **not** happen there.

Like in the Garden of Eden; it's **not** that Adam and Eve couldn't have gotten sick or hurt, but had they not sinned, they simply wouldn't have gotten sick or hurt.

It's **not** likely that there is any waste on the New Earth. It could be that when we drink of the water of life, or consume fruit from the tree of life, our glorified bodies will totally digest every bit of it, and have no elimination of waste.

The most amazing thing about the new eternal city is that **God's throne,** and that of the Lamb will be **relocated** to the New Jerusalem, so that God can live with His people.

Ezekiel 37: 27-28 says: *My tabernacle also shall be with them: yea, I will be their God, and they shall be my people. And the heathen shall know that I the Lord do sanctify Israel, when my sanctuary shall be in the midst of them for evermore.* This long awaited prophecy that Satan tried so hard to foil, will finally be confirmed.

Rev.22: 5 even without the sun or moon, there will be no night there, or need of artificial light. The glory of the Lord God gives them light. Evidently sleep will not be necessary for resurrected immortal beings.

Children will **not** be born there. *Matt. 22:30* Jesus said *"For in the resurrection they neither marry, nor are given in marriage, but are as the angels of God in heaven."*

As the bride of Christ, our total devotion will be to Jesus Christ our Savior. There will be no interest or desire to be married to anyone else who lives there. Not even our former spouse. It's not likely that there will be genders there. We will love everyone there equally.

Verse 5 also says: *The resurrected saints will reign **on** the New Earth forever,* but over whom, or what will they reign?

Apparently, the saints will reign over the New Earth itself to subdue it, and maintain it, much like Adam and Eve were instructed to do *Gen.1:28*. However, we will do it without satanic interference.

Since there are many languages spoken on earth, one might wonder how many languages will be spoken in heaven. Probably only one, and it will most likely be Hebrew; based on *Acts 26:12-14*. KJV

On the Damascus road Paul heard ***a voice from heaven*** say to him ***in the Hebrew tongue*** *"Saul, Saul, why do you persecute me? It is hard for thee to kick against the pricks."*

The New Earth will probably have abundant life (including tame animals), and will need continuous maintenance. His servants will be delighted to do whatever is necessary to keep the New Earth productive and beautiful. Fatigue and weariness will not be an issue there. Animals in heaven will **not** originate from this earth; but will more likely be part of the creation of the New Earth.

Rev.19: 14 speaks of horses in heaven; it says: *the armies which were in heaven followed Him upon white horses, clothed in fine linen, white and clean.* Since heaven will be an extension of the millennial reign of Christ, we can probably include the tame animals spoken of in *Isaiah 11: 6-9*

Isaiah 11: 6-9 (Paraphrased) *The wolf shall dwell with the lamb, and the leopard shall lie down with the kid; and the calf and the young lion together; and a little child shall lead them. The cow and the bear shall feed; their young ones shall lie down together: and the lion shall eat straw like the ox. The sucking child shall play on the hole of the asp. They shall not hurt or destroy in all my holy mountain: the earth shall be full of the knowledge of the Lord, as the waters cover the sea.*

Rev.22: 8-9 Again, John is so overwhelmed that he mistakenly falls down before the feet of the angel to worship. Again the angel immediately tells him, ***"Do not do it!*** I am a fellow servant; ***Worship God!"*** (John made the same mistake in C*h.19:10*)

John has made a huge mistake in worshipping anyone other than God. He has broken the First Commandment, not once but twice, and yet ***God knows*** John's faithful heart and ***understands*** that John was simply overwhelmed by all that he has seen. Isn't it nice to know that God knows our faithful heart, and He understands our human weaknesses when life is overwhelming?

Even So, Come, Lord Jesus

Rev.22: 10-11 in the last days there will come a time when it will be too late to repent. Repentance will no longer be an option. Any decisions made to accept or reject Jesus will be fixed forever. All that remains are rewards and consequences. As spiritual beings we will always exist somewhere; either heaven or hell.

Rev.22: 12-13 No one can be saved by good works, but our heavenly rewards can be based on our faithful service, and obedience to Jesus. He is the author and finisher of our faith.

Rev.22: 14 -16 *for those who trust and obey there will be complete access to the tree of life, and full freedom to enter and leave, and return to the magnificent eternal city of God. Jesus is the bright, morning star* (the new beginning) in whom we place our eternal hope.

Rev.22: 17 *the spirit of the bride, says, come. And let him that heareth say, come. And let him that is athirst come, and whosoever will, let him take the water of life freely.*

The invitation is given to all who inhabit the New Heaven, the New Earth, and the New Jerusalem to come, and take of the water of life freely. We will be constantly refreshed.

Rev.22: 18, A very stern warning is given to anyone who would attempt to alter the word of God with the intention of changing its' prophetic message. *God will **add** to them the plagues that are written in this book.*

Rev.22: 19 If anyone attempts to **take away** from the words of this book anything that would change its' prophetic message, *he will be denied access to the Book of Life, the holy city, and the promises and blessings that are written in this book.*

That doesn't mean that there shouldn't be different versions of the Bible, but none of them should change the prophetic, or doctrinal message of God's word.

Rev.22: 20 John hears Jesus' final reminder as He says *"Surely I come quickly."*

John might be recounting all the horrific things he has seen and heard in this awesome prophetic vision of things that must be hereafter

Rev.4:1, and yet his response is a robust welcome as he declares *"Even so, come, Lord Jesus."*

Rev.22: 21 The final benediction (blessing) is this: *"The grace of our Lord Jesus Christ be with you all. Amen."*

www.ingramcontent.com/pod-product-compliance
Lightning Source LLC
LaVergne TN
LVHW041947070526
838199LV00051BA/2934